Understanding *Tzniut*

Modern Controversies
in the Jewish Community

UNDERSTANDING *TZNIUT*

MODERN CONTROVERSIES
IN THE JEWISH COMMUNITY

RABBI YEHUDA HENKIN

URIM PUBLICATIONS
Jerusalem • New York

Understanding *Tzniut:* Modern Controversies in the Jewish Community
by Rabbi Yehuda Henkin
Copyright © 2008 by Rabbi Yehuda Henkin

With minor changes, Chapters One, Two, Five and part of Three, initially
appeared in *Tradition* magazine. Chapter Four appeared in *Hakirah*.

Layout design by Satya Levine
Printed at Hemed Press, Israel. First Edition.
ISBN-13: 978-965-524-005-4
ISBN-10: 965-524-005-3

Urim Publications
P.O. Box 52287, Jerusalem 91521 Israel

Lambda Publishers Inc.
3709 13th Avenue Brooklyn, New York 11218 U.S.A.
Tel: 718-972-5449 Fax: 718-972-6307, mh@ejudaica.com

www.UrimPublications.com

❧ Dedicated by members of the United Orthodox Synagogues of Houston ❦

Roger and Evelyn Medvin
in honor of our children, Sara and Seth

Michael and Susan Abramowitz
In memory of a lover of Zion, Gertrude Nutkiss, *z"l*

Mr. and Mrs. Max Reichenthal
in honor of our children, Nathan, Jaclyn and Ariel

Nava and Gideon Miller
in honor of our son Yair's Bar Mitzva

Drs. William and Sharon Lipsky
in memory of mother Gertrude Nutkis

Dena and Baruch Brody
in Memory of Samuel (Shea) Grosser

Gabrielle and Barry Gelman
in memory of Klara Dlugopiat

Atara and Ari Segal
in memory of Susan Jane Segal, *z"l*

Carole and Wesley Ashendorf
in honor of their children and grandchildren

CONTENTS

PART II

PART I

CHAPTER ONE

UNDERSTANDING *TZNIUT*

TODAY, THE ISSUE of *tzniut* – Jewish standards of modesty in dress and behavior, particularly as they relate to women – is at the focus of renewed public interest. In this essay I will examine the key Talmudic *sugyot* and *halachot* regarding *tzniut* in the hope of clarifying this much-discussed but little-understood area of Halachah.

A.   THE *SUGYA* IN *BERACHOT*

In *Berachot* 24a:

> R. Yitzchak said: "An [uncovered] *tefach* (handbreadth) in a woman is *ervah* (nakedness)." Regarding what [did R. Yitzchak say this]? If in regard to looking [at women], did not R. Sheshet say: "…Anyone who gazes even at a woman's little finger is as if he gazes at her private parts"? Rather, [R. Yitzchak said it] regarding one's wife and reading the *Shema*.
>
> R. Chisda said: "A woman's leg (*shok*) is *ervah*, as it is written (Isaiah 47:2), 'Reveal your leg (*shok*), pass over rivers,' and it is also written (v. 3), 'Your *ervah* will be uncovered and your shame will also be revealed.'"

Shmuel[1] said: "A woman's voice is *ervah*, as it is written (*Shir ha-Shirim* 2:14) '...for your voice is pleasant and your appearance is attractive.'"

R. Sheshet said: "A woman's hair is *ervah*, as it is written (4:1) 'Your hair resembles a herd of goats....'"

Tefach

R. Yitzchak did not need to forbid gazing lasciviously at women, for that was already prohibited (as per R. Sheshet) with regard to even less than a *tefach*. Rather, "regarding his wife and reading the *Shema*" prohibits reciting the *Shema* in the presence of a usually covered but currently uncovered (and therefore provocative) *tefach*, whether gazed at or not. This can be understood in two ways:

1. *Even* in the case of one's wife, a *tefach* or more is forbidden, and all the more so in other women, a *tefach* or more is forbidden – but less than a *tefach* is permitted.

2. *Only* in the case of one's wife is less than a *tefach* permitted, but in other women any uncovered area at all that is usually covered is forbidden – even less than a *tefach*.

The first view is that of R. Hai Gaon and R. Yonah,[2] *Sefer Yere'im*,[3] *Semag*,[4] *Semak*,[5] *Etz Chayim*,[6] *Sefer ha-Meorot*,[7] R. Manoach,[8] *Orchot Chayim*,[9]

---

[1] Shmuel belonged to the first generation of *amoraim*, while R. Yitzchak, R. Chisda and R. Sheshet lived in the second and third generations. Shmuel's pronouncement, "A woman's voice is *ervah*," thus preceded those about *tefach*, *shok* and hair. Why? Perhaps because the prohibition of voice is the least obvious of the four: *kol* is non-visual and not easily subsumed under *velo yir'eh becha ervat davar*, "and [G-d] shall not see a matter of *ervah* in you" (*Devarim* 23:15 and see below, "*Ervat Davar*"); see *Sefer Raviah*, no. 76. For that very reason it was necessary specifically to proclaim its *ervah* status, even before the others. (But see *Or Zarua* pt. 1, no. 133, who attributes the statement on hair to Shmuel and on voice to R. Sheshet, *pace* the partial emendation there.)

Raeh,[10] *Ohel Moed*[11] and *Tur*.[12] The second view is that of *Halachot Gedolot*,[13] R. Chananel,[14] Raviah,[15] *Sefer ha-Eshkol*,[16] *Or Zarua*,[17] *Hagahot Maimoniot*[18] and possibly Rosh.[19] *Shulchan Aruch* and many major commentators rule according to the first view.[20]

---

[2] R. Yonah to Rif, *Berachot* chap. 3 (p. 33), *s.v. ervah*, *"ve-hu ha-din le-chol ishah ha-megalah tefach."*

[3] *Sefer Yere'im ha-Shalem*, 392, *"de-afilu ishto ki megalah tefach minah asur likro kriat shema ke-negdah."*

[4] *Mitzvot Aseh* 18: *"Tefach be-ishah ervah... ve-lo yikra af al pi she-hi ishto."*

[5] Mitzvah 83, *"tefach be-ishah ve-afilu hi ishto."*

[6] *Hilchot Kriat Shema*, chap. 3, *"kol tefach be-ishah afilu be-ishto ervah."*

[7] Com. to *Berachot* 25a, *"Ve-tefach be-ishah... afilu be-ishto u-le-kriat shema."*

[8] *Sefer ha-Menuchah, Hilchot Kriat Shema* 3:16: *"Tefach meguleh mi-guf ha-ishah harei hu ke-tzoah... ve-davka tefach, aval pachot mi-tefach lav klum hu."*

[9] *Hilchot Kriat Shema*, par. 36, *"Kal guf ha-ishah ervah afilu hi ishto. Im roeh mimenah tefach meguleh lo yikra ke-negdah."* Also in *Sefer Kolbo* by the same author, chap. 10.

[10] Commentary to *Berachot* 24a. (p. 52): *"Tefach be-ishah ervah... le-inyan kriat shema ve-afilu be-ishto."*

[11] *Ma'arechet Tamid* 5:5 (p. 49a), *"Tefach meguleh... harei hu ke-ervah ve-afilu be-ishto asur likrot et hashema ke-negdah."*

[12] *Tur Orach Chayim* 75, *"Tefach ha-meguleh be-ishah... assur likrot kriat shema ke-negdah afilu hi ishto."*

[13] Cited in *Sefer Raviah*, par. 75, and other *rishonim*, but not found in our editions of *Halachot Gedolot*.

[14] Cited in *Sefer Raviah*, *loc cit*.

[15] *Ibid.*

[16] *Sefer haEshkol* (ed. Auerbach), pt. 1, chap. 7 (p. 15).

[17] Pt. 1, no. 133.

[18] In *Hilchot Kriat Shema*, chap. 3, letter *samech*. This view is commonly cited as that of *Hagahot Maimoniot*, but his language is from Raviah. I have not cited Rambam because of controversy over what his opinion is; see *Bet Yosef* and *Bach* in *Tur, Orach Chayim* 75; *Lechem Mishneh* in *Hilchot Kriat Shema*, *loc. cit.*; and at length in *Bnei Tzion* (Lichtman), (vol. 2) 75:1.

[19] *Berachot* 3:37. Cf. Rosh's wording *"ha le-acheret ha le-ishto"* with *Or Zarua*.

[20] *Orach Chayim* 75:1, *Levush, Bach, Eliyahu Rabbah, Shulchan Aruch ha-Rav* and, *Aruch ha-Shulchan, et al*, but see *Pri Chadash, Taz* and *Pri Megadim* 75:1 in *Mishbetzot Zahav*. Rema cites the second view as an additional opinion but does not decide between

Ervat Davar

In *Devarim* 23:15 it is written: "…*ve-lo yir'eh becha ervat davar*" (so that [G-d] will not see in you a matter (*davar*) of nakedness). The Sages expounded *davar* as *dibbur* (speech),[21] and the verse is taken to mean that *kriat Shema* and other spoken matters of *kedushah* may not be recited when human genitalia (*ervah*) are exposed.[22] Since the verse does not state "*velo tir'eh*" (*you* shall not see) but "*velo yir'eh*" (one who looks,[22a] i.e., G-d, shall not see), *kriat Shema* is proscribed by Torah law if actual *ervah* is uncovered, even if the person reciting *Shema* is blind or his eyes are closed and he does not see it.

Non-genital but provocative parts of the body, however, are *ervah* only rabbinically, and it is to this category that an uncovered *tefach* belongs. *Shok*, hair and voice will be discussed below.

---

them, and *Bach* and *Eliyahu Rabah* wrote that Rema agrees with the first view. *Chayei Adam* 4:2 in *Nishmat Adam* wrote that "all the *poskim*" follow the first view. Many *acharonim* rule that a married woman must cover all her hair, see below, but do not necessarily accept the second view concerning less than an uncovered *tefach*. Others hold that although the first view is primary, it is advisable where possible to pay heed to the second; see *Kaf ha-Chayim* in *Orach Chayim* 75, par. 10.

21 *Shabbat* 150a and Rashi; *Yerushalmi Terumot* 1:1, and see *Alei Tamar* on the *Yerushalmi, ad. loc.*

22 The syntax is difficult: the Torah could have written *devar ervah,* but what is *ervat davar,* literally "an *ervah* of a matter (or word)"? Perhaps *ervah* here has the connotation of shame, i.e., there shall not be a recitation of *Shema* made shameful by exposed genitalia. However, in the only other Biblical use of *ervat davar*, in the adjacent *Devarim* 24:1 "*ki matza bah ervat davar*" concerning grounds for divorce, none of this applies, and see *Sifrei* and *Midrash Tana'im* there and in 23:15. It may be that the exposition of *davar/dibbur* is only an *asmachta* peg for a wholly rabbinical prohibition; this would explain why Rambam omitted "*ve-haya machanecha kadosh, ve-lo yir'eh becha ervat davar*" from *Sefer ha-Mitzvot*; cf. Ramban, *Hosafot le-Mitzvot Lo Ta'aseh* 11.

22a "*Ve-lo yir'eh ha-ro'eh,*" Rashba, *Berachot* 24a. "*Ve-lo yir'eh*" can also be vocalized "*ve-lo yera'eh*" (it shall not be seen), to the same effect. Remarkably, however, although implicit in *Berachot* 25b, "*Ve-lo yir'eh becha ervat davar – ve-ha ke-mitchazia,*" neither reading is explicit anywhere in Talmudic literature.

The Torah prohibition does not depend on *hirhur* (sexual thoughts), since a male may not recite *Shema* when the genitals of other males or even his own alone are visible, even though there is normally no *hirhur* among men, and similarly for women among themselves. Rabbinical *ervah*, however, is linked to *hirhur*.[23]

The Length of a *Tefach*

A *tefach* is nominally a one-dimensional measurement of length corresponding to a handbreadth, i.e., the width of a palm. It is located by various *acharonim* at different points on a scale between eight and 10.4 centimeters.[24] *Tefach be-ishah*, however, refers to a two-dimensional surface area having both length and width (or breadth). There are at least three ways to define such a *tefach*:

1. A strip a *tefach* long, of any width.[25] In practice this amounts to a one-dimensional measurement, taken *le-chumra:* if either the length or width of the section exposed is a *tefach*, it is considered *ervah*.

2. An uncovered patch the area of a square *tefach* (*tefach al tefach*).[26] According to the various calculations of a *tefach*, this would range from 64 cm² to 108.16 cm.² This area can be measured as 1 x 1 *tefachim* or as 2 x 1/2, 3 x 1/3, and so

---

[23] Ravad as cited by *Sefer ha-Hashlamah*, *Sefer ha-Meorot* and *Rashba* to *Berachot* 24a; *Sefer ha-Menuchah* and *Sefer ha-Batim* in *Hilchot Kriat Shema*, *loc. cit*; Raviah and others. See also below, note 196.

[24] See *Encyclopedia Talmudit*, *s.v. amah, tefach*. The most widely accepted measure, which is the Jerusalem *minhag* and that of my grandfather *z"l* and was the measure used by Rambam, is eight centimeters. There are many who use a higher figure *le-chumra* but not *le-kula*. Surprisingly, R. Falk (see below, note 43) cites ten centimeters, a round number corresponding to no one's calculation and which represents a marked *kula* relative to eight centimeters.

[25] Resp. *Mekadshei ha-Shem*, no. 97. The responsum is by the author of Resp. *Mishneh Sachir* and *Eim ha-Banim Semeichah*.

[26] But see *Niddah* 26a: "We said a *tefach*, not a *tefach al tefach*!"

forth.[27] Even if one of the dimensions is more than a *tefach*, if the total area is less than that of a square *tefach* it is not *ervah*.

3. An uncovered area of which both length and width are at least a *tefach*. In practice this, too, amounts to a one-dimensional measurement, but *le-kula*.[28] If either length or width is *not* a *tefach*, it is not considered *ervah*.

According to the first definition, the area of *tefach be-ishah* can be less than a square *tefach;* according to the second it is exactly that of a square *tefach;* while according to the third definition, even more than a square *tefach* may still not be *tefach be-ishah*.

Support for the third definition can be brought from an adjacent *sugya*. In *Berachot* 23b the Sages discuss the maximum amount one should uncover oneself when on the toilet for purposes of *tzniut*. 'One source taught: when he relieves himself he uncovers a *tefach* in back and two *tefachim* in front, while another source taught, a *tefach* in back and nothing in front."[29] Manifestly, this does not mean uncovering an area of only one or two square handbreadths. These are not large enough – certainly not the 8 x 8=64 cm² (9.91 sq. inch) measurement, and not even the 108.16 cm² figure – not to mention the impossibility of maneuvering one's clothing in exactly the requisite way.

Rather, the Gemara is describing a person who uncovers himself by pulling down or pulling up his garments a distance of one or two *tefachim* all along his front or back, even though this reveals much more than a square *tefach* or two. This is called an uncovered *tefach* regarding *tzniut* in the toilet,

---

[27] Resp. *Igrot Moshe, Even ha-Ezer* vol. 1, no. 58, takes it for granted that 2 x ½ = one *tefach* for the purpose of head covering.

[28] This applies in the case of a covered area adjacent to an uncovered area, such as along the neckline, but not in the case of a hole or "window" in the clothing, etc.

[29] The Gemara explains that the two sources reflect anatomical differences between men and women.

and we can apply it to an uncovered *tefach* regarding *tzniut* in women, a page later in the Gemara.

If this third definition of *tefach* is used, few of the necklines women normally wear today expose a *tefach*.

Shok

Why was *shok*, of all the parts of the body, singled out by R. Chisda for special mention? There are several possibilities:

1. One might think that *shok* is not *ervah* at all.[30] R. Chisda therefore clarifies that *tefach be-ishah ervah* applies to a woman's *shok*, the same as to other parts of her body that are normally covered.

2. According to R. Chisda, the law regarding *shok* is more stringent than it is regarding other parts of the body. In s*hok*, even less than an uncovered *tefach* is *ervah*.[31]

---

[30] Either because a woman's *shok* is occasionally uncovered (Raeh, R. Avraham Alshvili, *Shitah Mekubetzet*); or because the parallel limb in a male is not a place of *tzniut* and need not be covered (Ravad and others); or because a woman's *shok* is frequently soiled and one might think it is not an object of desire (*Bach*).

The latter two explanations raise questions. First, there are other parts of the body that are *tzanua* in a woman and not in a man, such as the abdomen, and see *Shir ha-Shirim* 6:3, "your belly is like a mound of wheat." Why single out *shok*? Also, according to *Bach*'s explanation, the prohibition of gazing at a woman's *shok* could not be learned from the prohibition of gazing at her little finger, for although a finger is smaller it is also cleaner, and so there is no *kal ve-chomer*. Why, then, expound that an uncovered *shok* prevents the recitation of *Shema*? Perhaps R. Chisda only meant that gazing at a woman's *shok* is prohibited in spite of its being sullied.

However, it can be countered that R. Chisda's citation of the verses in Isaiah linking *shok* with *ervah*, which in turn evokes *ve-lo yir'eh becha ervat davar* that the Sages expound as referring to *kriat Shema*, shows that R. Chisda, too, is referring to *kriat Shema*.

[31] *Bach* and *Pri Megadim*, *loc. cit.* Each interprets the *chumra* according to his own view: for *Bach*, who holds that an uncovered *tefach be-ishah* applies equally to one's wife and

---

17

3. By citing Isaiah, R. Chisda indicates that the Halachic status of *shok* is unchangeable.[32] Since Scripture explicitly links *shok* with *ervah*, it will always rabbinically have the status of *ervah* even in a climate or society where women go about with exposed thighs.

Possibilities 1 and 2 are mutually exclusive since those who explain R. Chisda as stating that *shok* is *like* other covered parts cannot also be saying that *unlike* other parts, even less than a *tefach* of *shok* is forbidden. *Rishonim* who cite possibility 1 are *Sefer ha-Eshkol*, Ravad, *Sefer ha-Hashlamah*, *Sefer ha-Meorot*, *Sefer ha-Batim*, Raeh, Rashba and, apparently, *Tur*. Possibility 2 is found in the *acharonim*. Rambam and *Shulchan Aruch* make no separate mention of *shok*, indicating that they, too, view it as the same as other parts of the body. Rif deleted the entire *sugya*.[33]

Location of *Shok*

R. Chisda's proof-text is from Isaiah (47:2–3):

Take millstones and grind flour; reveal [your] plait, expose [your] hem (*chespi shoval*), reveal [your] *shok*, cross rivers. Your *ervah* will be revealed and your disgrace will be visible.

Although *shok* is not explicitly labeled *ervah*, the two are clearly linked. Note that in verse 2 all the verbs are in the imperative, "take" (*kechi*),

---

to other women, less than a *tefach* is *ervah* only in the case of *shok*. *Pri Megadim*, on the other hand, wrote according to the view of *Hagahot Maimoniot* that in other women even less than a *tefach* is *ervah*; *shok* is just an example, and less than a *tefach* is considered *ervah* in other covered parts of the body as well.

[32] *Sefer haEshkol*, loc. cit.: "Because Scripture calls [*shok*] *ervah*, it involves *ve-lo yir'eh becha ervat davar*," i.e., its status cannot be changed. This would equally apply to female breasts, which are linked by Scripture to *eryah* (=*ervah*) in Ezekiel 16:7: "…your breasts are formed and your [pubic] hair is growing and you are naked and *eryah*." It would therefore be forbidden to recite *Shema* in the presence of uncovered breasts even in places or among tribes where women go bare-breasted in public.

[33] See Ravad quoted in *Sefer ha-Meorot* and Rashba.

"expose" (*chespi*) and "reveal" (*gali*), while verse 3 is in the passive future tense, "will be revealed" (*tigal*) and "will be visible" (*tiraeh*). I think the inference is clear: if she uncovers her *shok* her *ervah* will then be revealed, even if unintentionally. *Shok* and actual *ervah* are adjacent to each other, and uncovering one will result in uncovering the other. This may be the meaning of R. Avraham Alshvili and *Shitah Mekubetzet* in *Berachot* 24a who wrote, "Although occasionally [*shok*] is revealed, it has the status of a covered area of the body because it leads to [uncovering the actual] *ervah*."

It also supports the ruling that *shok* with regard to *ervah* refers to a woman's upper leg, above and not below the knee,[34] for the lower leg is not adjacent to *ervah* and uncovering it will not result in uncovering *oto makom*. Isaiah's depiction of a woman exposing her *shok* in order to cross rivers (*neharot*)[35] is further indication that *shok* is above the knee: were it below the knee and she was clothed down to her ankles to cover it, she would have to raise her skirts to cross even a puddle. The only reference in Scripture to a woman's *shok*, then, appears to refer to her upper leg, as opposed to Talmudic usage where it invariably means the leg below the knee.[36]

The above helps explain *tefach be-ishah ervah* as well. As opposed to *shok*, hair and voice, an uncovered *tefach* has no Scriptural peg; R. Yitzchak in

---

[34] *Mishnah Berurah* on 75:1, and see *Chazon Ish, Orach Chayim,* chap. 16, no. 8. Resp. *Igrot Moshe, Even ha-Ezer,* part 4, no. 100 (6) takes this view as a given. However, it remains the subject of controversy.

[35] *Neharot* are rivers, as opposed to *nechalim* (streams). See also Radak in 47:2, *s.v. chespi shoval,* who cites *Midrash Chazit* as interpreting *shoval* as the turbulent or strongly-flowing part of the river (*shibolet ha-nahar*) as in Psalms 69:3. This cannot likely be crossed by lifting one's garments only up to the knees.

Radak himself explains *shok* as being the lower leg in Judges 15:8. But I think there is no Scriptural proof that this is so; see *Devarim* 28:35; Psalms 147:10; Song of Songs 15:5; and Proverbs 26:7, all of which can be interpreted as referring to either above or below the knee. Even *shok al yerech* in Judges is idiomatic and *al* can mean "next to," lending itself to other interpretations. [R. Yosef Kra, a younger contemporary of Rashi, also identified the *shok* in Isaiah as the "upper thigh" (*yerach ha-elyonah*).]

[36] See Mishnah *Ohalot* 1:8; *Nidah* 8:1 (57b), *et al.*

Berachot offers no source for it. It may, rather, be a *gezerah*. *Ervah* is the quintessential covered part of the body; sexual relations are euphemized as *gilui ervah*, uncovering the always-covered genital region. Since parts of the body that are always covered resemble *ervah* in this regard, the Sages prohibited reciting *Shema* when those parts are uncovered, just as in the case of actual *ervah*, regardless of whether or not *hirhur* is present.[37]

Kriat Shema or Divrei Torah

Shema is paradigmatic of all prayers and blessings: none may be recited in the presence of uncovered *ervah* of even rabbinical nature. Is studying Torah permitted in such circumstances? *Sefer Yere'im*[38] forbids it, and for that reason relies on *"et la'asot la-Shem"* for a dispensation to permit Torah study within earshot of the songs of Gentile women; he is cited by a number of *rishonim*.[39] All the more so, this applies to *tefach*.

However, others disagree. Meiri wrote in *Berachot* 24a:

> Viewing a *tefach* in his wife that is normally not exposed prohibits *kriat Shema* but does not prohibit *divrei Torah*, since seeing causes *hirhur*.[40]

This is also the opinion of *Sefer ha-Hashlamah*,[41] who records an additional sentence that apparently was in his text of the Gemara:

---

[37] See below, note 196.

[38] *Loc. cit. Sefer Yere'im* views *kol be-ishah* as rabbinically the same as actual *ervah*, similar to *tefach*. A *davar she-bi-kedushah* may not be said if such singing is audible, even if those present pay no attention to it.

[39] *Mordechai, loc. cit. Piskei Rikanti* quotes *Sefer Yere'im*, but does not explicitly refer to studying Torah.

[40] In contrast to *Sefer Yere'im*, Meiri views the prohibition of reciting a *davar she-bi-kedushah* facing an exposed *tefach* as being solely because of *hirhur*. But Torah is itself the antidote to *hirhur*, as in *Kiddushin* 30b, "I created the evil inclination, [but] I created Torah as an antidote"; and see *Bnei Banim*, vol. 2, p. 162.

[41] *Loc cit. Sefer Rokeach*, as well, wrote that when facing *ervah* it is forbidden to "recite the *Shema* and pray," and did not mention Torah study.

> Did not R. Sheshet say, "Anyone who gazes even at a woman's little finger is as if he gazes at her private parts"? Rather, regarding his wife. [But] in *divrei Torah*, why not? Rather, regarding his wife and reading the *Shema*.

This is important support for permitting men to lecture on Torah and *mussar* to audiences that include women who are improperly dressed.[42]

Halachah: *Tefach* and *Shok*

An uncovered area of less than a *tefach* of normally-covered parts of the body, including *shok*, is not considered *ervah* and does not impede the recital of the *Shema* and other matters of *kedushah*. This is the view of most *rishonim*, the *Shulchan Aruch* and many major *acharonim*. And while any community is entitled to set more rigorous standards and make them obligatory on its members, it cannot bind members of other communities or even those who do not belong to any community.

The above is in opposition to the recent work *Oz ve-Hadar Levushah*[43] by Rabbi Eliyahu Falk, who prohibits a blouse whose top button is slightly too low and where some skin on the collarbone is visible below what can be considered the neck, but much less than a *tefach*:

> All areas that must be covered... must be covered completely. There is absolutely no *heter* for a woman to leave less than a *tefach* of those areas uncovered... even a minor exposure is provocative and a serious shortcoming in *tznius*. It is therefore *ossur* for the neckline of the garment to extend even half a centimeter beyond the permitted level. (Sources: *OC* 75:1 in Rema; *Chazon Ish OC,* 16:7; *Iggros Moshe, EH* 1:58, *s.v. Ve-lachen*.)

---

[42] See *Chazon Ish, Orach Chayim* 11:8.

[43] Rabbi Pesach Eliyahu Falk, *Oz ve-Hadar Levushah: Modesty, an Adornment for Life — Halachos and Attitudes Concerning Tznius of Dress and Conduct* (Feldheim, 1998), p. 218.

I wonder what provocation there is in an exposed half-centimeter and whether Rabbi Falk is not defining it into existence: if the neckline is too low, *ipso facto* it must provoke. As for the sources provided, Rema merely cites, as a second opinion, the view of *Hagahot Maimoniot* that even less than a *tefach* is forbidden, and according to some authorities Rema himself disagrees. What Rabbi Falk is referring to is not Rema but rather Rema as construed by *Chazon Ish*, which is not the same thing.

The arguments on the issue in *Chazon Ish* are far from decisive, in my opinion,[44] and his conclusion rests on the assumption that concerning a prohibited part of a woman "no seeing is possible [of less than a *tefach*] without [forbidden] gazing," an assumption that does not appear to be shared by the *rishonim*.[45] As for Resp. *Igrot Moshe* at the location cited,[46] unlike *Chazon Ish* he distinguishes between seeing and gazing, and although he explains the view of *Hagahot Maimoniot* he does not specifically endorse it.

Upper Arm (*Zeroa*)

The upper arm is not mentioned separately[47] in *Berachot* 24b. However, Rashi in Isaiah 47:2 describes both *shok* and *zeroa* as limbs that a woman normally covers,[48] and *Sefer Rokeach* wrote:

---

[44] See *Bnei Banim* vol. 4, *maamar* 3 (3).

[45] See the *rishonim* cited in notes 9–18 above, and in particular R. Manoach, "in a woman's body… less than a *tefach* has no significance" (*lav klum hu*).

[46] There are a number of responsa in *Igrot Moshe* on this issue. See *Bnei Banim*, vol. 3, no. 25 (5) and below, "Denying *Igrot Moshe*."

[47] See *Tiferet Shmuel* (37) on the Rosh in *Berachot*: "Women who regularly uncover their upper arms and they regularly are open until near their nipples (*regilin lihiyot patuach ad samuch le-dadeha*), I apply to them [the Scriptural phrase] '*chukim lo tovim*,' and 'a *tefach* in a woman is *ervah*.'" It is unclear whether he refers to sleeveless dresses that permit the body to be seen around the arms as in the *Korban ha-Edah* cited below (next section), or what seems more likely, to the European fashion in the seventeenth and eighteenth centuries of extremely low necklines. In any case, the principle of 'a *tefach* in a woman is *ervah*" is the yardstick.

[48] *S.v. tzamatech*. He does not equate *zeroa* with *shok* except insofar as both are usually covered. Rashi's other views on *shok* are not known, other than that apparently he

22

> Hair, whether of his wife or another woman, or her *shok,* or
> a *tefach* of her skin or when her upper arms are uncovered
> (*zero'oteha megulot*) – he is forbidden to recite *Shema* or pray
> [facing her].[49]

Acharonim derived from this that *zeroa* has the same Halachic status as *shok.*[50] I am surprised at this, for close examination of *Rokeach* yields a different conclusion. Note that he changed the order of the Gemara and began with hair and *shok* followed by *tefach,* rather than listing *tefach* first; the implication is that *tefach,* mentioned only afterwards, does not apply either to *shok*[51] or hair. But he also did not write "a *tefach* of her skin or her upper arms" but rather "a *tefach* of her skin or when her upper arms are uncovered," i.e., *tefach* does not apply to the *zeroa* either, which has its own measure: that of being uncovered. We are constrained to interpret this as being *le-kula,* as referring to uncovering most of the limb, for if more than fifty percent of the upper arm is covered it certainly cannot be deemed "uncovered."

Zero'oteha megulot is the same regarding *kriat Shema* as it is regarding *dat Yehudit,* the binding customs of modest Jewish women. Thus, in *Ketubbot* 72b, "R. Yehuda said that Shmuel said, '[*dat Yehudit* is violated] if she displays her upper arms to people.'" And in *Gittin* 90a[52]:

> This is characteristic of a bad person: he sees his wife going
> out with uncovered head, and she knits in the market place
> and [her dress is] open (*u-frumah*) on both sides... [and he
> does not remonstrate with her].

---

views both *tefach* and *shok* as applying to *eshet ish* and not to women in general; see *Einayim la-Mishpat* to *Berachot* 24a, par. 9 and *Sefer Bnei Tzion, loc. cit.*

[49] *Hilchot Tefilah,* chap. 324.

[50] *Eliyahu Rabbah* 75:3, *Chayei Adam* 4:2, *Mishnah Berurah* 75:2.

[51] He may be of the opinion that in *shok* even less than a *tefach* is forbidden. Concerning hair, see below.

[52] *Tosafot* in 90b, *s.v. Im bnei adam,* identify the discussion as concerning *dat Yehudit.*

Rashi explained that this is how Gentile women in France dressed, with flesh of their bodies visible around their armpits, and see Jeremiah 38:12. This is the meaning of the Jerusalem Talmud in *Gittin*[53]:

> From where do we know that [a woman] who goes out with her hair uncovered, her dress open on both sides and her upper arms exposed *(u-zero'oteha chalutzot)* [can be summarily divorced]?

Korban ha-Edah wrote in his second explanation:

> This refers to when her flesh is visible, and her upper arms have to be completely exposed. But if her sleeves are merely torn, although the flesh of her upper arms is visible, this is not immodesty *(pritzut)*.

It thus emerges from Rashi, *Yerushalmi* and *Korban ha-Edah* that *pritzut* in exposure of the upper arms comes not from the arms themselves but from the body being visible via the arms.[54] This, then, is what *Sefer Rokeach* means by *zero'oteha megulot,* the same language as *zero'oteha chalutzot* in the *Yerushalmi* This appears to be a powerful source for *limmud zechut* on behalf of otherwise modest women whose sleeves do not reach to their elbows.

A typology can be established according to this, as follows:

1. sleeveless dresses – forbidden by all opinions, as the body can be seen.

2. short sleeves, loose – forbidden if body can be seen.

3. short sleeves, tight – body cannot be seen, but prohibited if most of the upper arm is uncovered *(rubo k'kulo)*.

---

[53] Ch. 9, *halachah* 11.

[54] See above, note 47, and *Divrei Chamudot* on the Rosh in *Berachot*, chap, 3, par. 116. This makes perfect sense, for why should the faraway upper arms have the same stringency as thighs that are adjacent to actual *ervah*?

4. sleeves halfway to elbow – proscribed because of *tefach meguleh;* room for *limmud zechut.*

5. sleeves to within a *tefach* of the elbow – minimum permitted.

6. sleeves to elbow – recommended.

7. sleeves to below elbow – first-level *chumra.*

8. sleeves to wrists – second-level *chumra.*

The above does not supplant any communal or familial *minhag.*

Hair: Married and Unmarried Women

Girls and never-married women[55] are permitted to go about bareheaded, and men may recite *Shema* in their presence. There are two schools of thought concerning hair. The first is that of Rabbenu Tam[56] and others[57] who hold that unlike the statements regarding *tefach* and *shok,* the principle that "hair in a woman is *ervah*" does not prohibit men from reciting *Shema* but only warns them not to gaze at women's hair because of the likelihood of *hirhur.* This would explain why R. Sheshet said only "A woman's hair is *ervah*" but made no mention of *tefach.*

Following this, we might explain that there is nothing wrong with unmarried girls *(betulot)* going about bareheaded, for just as they need not cover their "little fingers," they need not cover their hair. The onus would be on the man not to gaze at their hair, just as it is his responsibility not to gaze at their fingers. But this is a false analogy: a woman's fingers are unobtrusive and not especially alluring. Hair, by contrast, is basic to a woman's good looks. Since hair is *ervah,* i.e., a source of *hirhur,* then regardless of the question of *kriat Shema,* why is the hair of unmarried women not a stumbling

---

[55] *Bet Shmuel* on *Even ha-Ezer* 21:3.

[56] Cited in *Piskei Rikanti, Orchot Chayim* and *Ohel Moed.* R. Tam specifically cites unmarried women as proof that *"se'ar be-ishah ervah"* is unconnected to *kriat Shema.*

[57] R. Yehuda b. Yitzchak *Sir Leon* (whose *Tosafot* are mislabeled *Tosfot R. Yehuda he-Chassid),* cited in *Or Zarua.* This is apparently the opinion of Rambam, as well, who mentions hair in *Hilchot Issurei Biah* 21:2 but not in *Hilchot Kriat Shema* 3:16.

block to men, particularly since today all post-pubertal girls are classified as *niddot*?[58]

The answer must be that because men are used to seeing the hair of unmarried women, they pay no attention to it and therefore there is no *hirhur*.

According to the second school of thought held by most *rishonim*, however, a married woman's uncovered hair does prevent a man from reciting the *Shema*, in a rabbinical extension of *"ve-lo yir'eh becha ervat davar."* This applies whether or not a man has *hirhur* in the specific case.[59] Nevertheless, concerning the hair of unmarried girls and women, Raviah wrote:

> All these things [mentioned above] as *ervah*, are only in things that are not normally uncovered *(ein regilut lehigalot)*. But we are not concerned about a maiden who normally goes about bareheaded, for there is no *hirhur*.[60]

According to this, as well, since men are used to seeing the hair of unmarried girls there is no *hirhur*.

Mishnah Berurah and *Aruch ha-Shulchan*

A fundamental disagreement concerning this issue can be found among *acharonim* from over a century ago. *Mishnah Berurah* wrote in chapter 75, paragraph 10:

---

[58] According to *Mishnah Berurah*, 75:7, *niddot* are in the category of *arayot*. However, this is the subject of considerable controversy, as is the related question of whether relations with a *niddah* are subject to *yehareg ve-al ya'avor*: see Rashi in *Sanhedrin* 73b, s.v. *apegama raba*; Ritva in *Pesachim* 25b vs. *Sefer ha-Chinuch*, no. 296; R. Tam in *Sefer ha-Yashar, chelek ha-teshuvot* no. 80; and *Tosafot* in *Gittin* 2b s.v. *havi* vs. Rashba in *Chulin* 10a. Also see Resp. *Pnei Yehoshua*, pt. 2, no. 44; *Maharsham* pt. 2, no. 182; *Avnei Nezer, Yoreh Deah* no. 12 (11) and 461(10); *Chelkat Yoav, Yoreh Deah* no. 29; and *Tzitz Eliezer*, vol. 17, no. 32 and vol. 20, no. 36 [and *Bnei Banim*, vol. 4 no. 7 (2–3)].

[59] See below, *"Lo plug"* and note 196.

[60] *Sefer Raviah, loc. cit.,* followed by *Mordechai*, Rosh and *Hagahot Maimoniot*.

Even if the way of this woman and her friends in that place is to go bareheaded in the market as immodest women do, it is forbidden [to recite *Shema* facing her uncovered hair], just as in the case of uncovering her *shok* which is forbidden under all circumstances... because she is required to cover her hair by law [and this involves a Torah prohibition...]. All daughters of Israel who hold fast to Mosaic practice (*dat Moshe*) from the days of our forefathers through today have been careful about this.

But *Aruch ha-Shulchan* disagreed:[61]

Come, let us decry the breaches [in observance] in our generations. Because of our many sins, for many years the daughters of Israel have been wanton in this transgression and they go about bareheaded. All the protests against it have proved futile; the plague has spread, and married women go about with their hair [uncovered] like *betulot*. Woe to us that this has happened in our day! However, in any event it seems that, by law, we are permitted to pray and recite blessings facing their uncovered heads, because nowadays most of them go about in this way and it has become like the normally uncovered parts of her body, as *Mordechai* wrote in the name of Raviah: "All these things mentioned above as *ervah*, are only in things that are not normally uncovered, but we are not concerned about a virgin

---

[61] *Orach Chayim* 75, par. 7. *Mishnah Berurah* on this section of *Orach Chayim* was published in 1892, and the parallel *Aruch ha-Shulchan* appeared in 1903. (*Aruch ha-Shulchan* on *Choshen Mishpat* was the first section to be printed, in 1874). *Aruch ha-Shulchan* cites *Mishnah Berurah* by name numerous times, such as in 11:2, 12:4, 25:23; 62:4 and 91:22. He cites *Mishnah Berurah* but rejects his views in 79:11 and 219:22. Often he disagrees with him without mentioning him by name, see *AH* 55:20 which is clearly a response to *MB* 55:52; *AH* 370:13 which responds to *MB* 370:27; and such is the case here as well. On the question of the authority of *Aruch ha-Shulchan* versus *Mishnah Berurah* see *Bnei Banim*, vol. 2, no. 8.

who normally goes about bareheaded, for there is no *hirhur.*"
Since with us even married women do so, it follows that
there is no *hirhur.*

According to *Mishnah Berurah,* parts of the body that must be covered by
law (as opposed to custom) do not lose their status as *ervah* even if all
women uncover them, regardless of whether or not *hirhur* is present.
According to *Aruch ha-Shulchan,* on the other hand, the absence or presence
of *hirhur* is determinative, and he cites *rishonim* to that effect. Indeed, Raviah,
Mordechai, Rosh and *Hagahot Maimoniot* all mention no factor other than
hirhur.

On the other hand, *Sefer ha-Batim* [62] seems to add a consideration similar
to that of *Mishnah Berurah*:

> There is someone who said that it is permitted [to recite
> *Shema*] while facing the *betulot* because such is their way [to
> go bareheaded], and her hair is like her face, hands and feet.
> But in a married woman, all of her hair in a place that should
> properly be covered *(ra'ui lehitkasot),* is *ervah.*

The wording "should properly" implies an imperative. According to this,
only in the case of unmarried girls who are under no obligation to cover
their hair can uncovered hair can be classed with hands, face and feet. *Shema*
may be recited facing them, but not in the case of married women who by
law must cover their hair.

Resp. *Igrot Moshe* [63] adduced support for *Aruch ha-Shulchan*'s position from
the Gemara, and see at length in Resp. *Yabia Omer.* [64] In practice, this ruling
of *Aruch ha-Shulchan* is widely relied upon. However, *Oz ve-Hadar Levushah*
makes no mention of it.

---

[62] *Hilchot Kriat Shema* 3:30. Cf. *Or Zarua,* pt. 1, no. 133.
[63] *Orach Chayim,* vol 1, no. 42.
[64] Vol. 6, *Orach Chayim,* no 13 (2–3, 5).

Types of Infractions

The gap between *Mishnah Berurah* and *Aruch ha-Shulchan* is narrower than it seems. *Aruch ha-Shulchan* describes a situation in which most women in most places go bareheaded, while *Mishnah Berurah* wrote concerning "this woman and her friends in that place," i.e., in a specific location. *Aruch ha-Shulchan* might agree with *Mishnah Berurah* on this.

More significantly, *Mishnah Berurah* refers only to violations of Torah law: "This involves a Torah prohibition.... All daughters of Israel who hold fast to Mosaic practice *(dat Moshe)*...." He does not mention infractions of merely Jewish practice *(dat Yehudit)*; concerning these, *Mishnah Berurah* could agree with *Aruch ha-Shulchan*.

This distinction is of importance because the arguments within many Orthodox communities today are not over married women going altogether bareheaded, which all agree is forbidden under *dat Moshe*. Rather, the controversy is over the parameters of *dat Yehudit,* and concerning this there is no stricture in *Mishnah Berurah* against taking local practice into account in permitting *kriat Shema* and *tefilah*.

B.   THE *SUGYA* IN *KETUBBOT*

In *Ketubbot* 72a–b:

> Mishnah: These [women] may be divorced without being paid their *ketubah*: a violator of *dat Moshe* and [*dat*] *Yehudit*. What is *dat Moshe*? If she feeds him untithed food, has relations with him when she is *niddah,* does not separate *challah*.... What is *dat Yehudit*? If she goes out bareheaded or knits in the marketplace and converses with everyone.

> Gemara: Isn't [going out] bareheaded a Torah violation (*de-oraita*), as it is written (*Bamidbar* 5:18): "[The priest] shall uncover the woman's head," and R. Yishmael's school taught [that this is] "a warning to the daughters of Israel not to go out bareheaded"? From the Torah, [wearing] a *kaltah* is

sufficient, but [according to] *dat Yehudit*, even a *kaltah* is [insufficient and] forbidden.

R. Asi said [that] R. Yochanan [said], "[Wearing] a *kaltah* does not constitute [going] bareheaded."

R. Zeirah[65] challenged him: "What location [is being referred to]? If in the market place, [wearing only a *kaltah*] is a violation of *dat Yehudit*. And if in a [private] courtyard, [if you require a *kaltah* there at all,] you will not have even one daughter of our forefather Abraham left married to her husband!"

Abaye, or perhaps R. Kahana, said: "[R. Asi is referring to when she goes] from courtyard to courtyard via a [semi-public] passageway."

Derivation from *Sotah*

A *sotah* – a woman suspected by her husband of infidelity – suffered the degradation of having her head uncovered before a throng of onlookers at the entrance to the Temple courtyard. This implies that prior to that her head had been covered. The Talmud learns from this that a married woman must cover her head.[66]

But perhaps all that can be learned is that women who approached the Temple grounds covered their heads out of respect there, but not elsewhere? Were that the case, however, there would be little humiliation involved in having her head covering removed. That the Torah considers it a humiliation indicates that women did not appear bareheaded in public.

---

[65] R. Asi's student, see *Pesachim* 106a.

[66] Alternatively, from the redundancy that the priest shall uncover "the woman's head" (and not simply "her head") we learn that that woman's head alone shall be uncovered, and not the heads of other women (Meiri).

Dat Moshe and *Dat Yehudit*

In my opinion, there are two different explanations of *dat Moshe* and *dat Yehudit* in the *rishonim:*

1. *Dat Moshe* refers to norms of *tzniut* mandated by the Torah, or at least to rabbinical edicts with a *semach* from the Torah,[67] while *dat Yehudit* includes those norms that originate in custom. This is explicit in Rashi,[68] Rambam,[69] *Semag,*[70] *Tosfot Rid,*[71] *Orchot Chayim,*[72] *Meiri,*[73] *Magid Mishneh*[74] and other *rishonim.*

2. Rosh,[75] however, wrote that a woman violated *dat Moshe* if she set a stumbling-block before her husband, already causing him to sin. By contrast, *Dat Yehudit* prohibits "brazen behavior [that arouses] the suspicion of promiscuity" *(chatzifuta ve-chashad zenut),* regardless of the provenance of the norm her behavior violates.

Rosh does not limit *dat Yehudit* to custom, nor do *Semak*[76] and *Tur,*[77] and it is likely that they all share the same approach. Rosh's definition resolves a

---

[67] Rambam as explained by *Terumat ha-Deshen, Teshuvah* no. 242, and see no. 10. According to this, the *gemara*'s question "Isn't [going] bareheaded *de-oraita?*" refers to a *remez* and not to an explicit law in the Torah. Cf. Meiri, "*dat Moshe* applies to commands written in the Torah or hinted in it."

[68] *Ketubbot* 72a, *s.v. dat Yehudit.*

[69] *Hilchot Ishut* 24:11–12.

[70] *Mitzvot 'Aseh* 48.

[71] *Ketubbot* 72a.

[72] Pt. 2, *Hilchot Ketubbot* par. 33.

[73] *Ketubbot* 72a.

[74] Comm. on Rambam, *loc. cit.*

[75] *Ketubbot* 3:27 (p. 28), and see *Bnei Banim,* vol. 3, no. 22, translated in my *Responsa on Contemporary Jewish Women's Issues* (Ktav, 2003), chap. 17 (henceforth referred to as *RoCJWI).*

[76] *Mitzvah* 28.

[77] *Orach Chayim* 115. The author of *Tur* was Rosh's son.

number of difficulties in the Mishnah and Gemara.[78] Nevertheless, most *rishonim* follow the first explanation that *dat Yehudit* is grounded in custom, and this is the view cited by the *acharonim*.

Time and Place

Rashi[79] defined *dat Yehudit* as practices adopted by Jewish women *(she-nahagu benot Yisrael)* that are not required by Scripture. A number of *rishonim* imply that these practices vary according to time and place. *Tosfot Rid*[80] wrote that while *dat Yehudit* does not inherently involve a prohibition, "women behave *(nohagot)* in such fashion as a way of *tzniut*," in the present tense; in other words, it depends on contemporary practice. *Semag*[81] wrote that *dat Yehudit* requires that a woman wear a shawl 'like all the other women" *(ki-she'ar kol ha-nashim)*; hence, if the others do not wear one, neither need she.

Moreover, Rambam is clear[82] that *dat Yehudit* varies from place to place. In *Hilchot Ishut* 24:12, he wrote:

> What is *dat Yehudit?* It is the modest behavior practiced by daughters of Israel. These are the things, that if she does [any] one of them, she has violated *dat Yehudit*. She goes out to the market place or in an open passageway and her head is uncovered and she is not wearing a *redid* (shawl) like all the women, even though her hair is covered with a kerchief.

Yet in 13:11, he wrote:

> [In] a place where their custom is that a woman does not go out to market with only a cap *(kippah)* on her head, until she wears a *redid* that covers all of her body like a *tallit,* [her husband] must give her a *redid*....

---

[78] See *Bnei Banim, ibid.* For instance, why does the Mishnah list going bareheaded only under *dat Yehudit* and not under *dat Moshe?*

[79] *Loc. cit.*

[80] *Ibid.*

[81] *loc. cit.*

[82] Cf. *Perishah* in *Even ha-Ezer* 115, sub. par. 10.

That same *redid* without which a woman violates *dat Yehudit* in chapter 24 is dependent on local custom in chapter 13.

R. Asi and R. Zeira

The end of the *sugya* seems to contradict the view that *dat Yehudit* varies according to local circumstances:

> R. Asi said [that] R. Yochanan [said], "[Wearing] a *kaltah* does not constitute [going] bareheaded."

> R. Zeira challenged him: "What location [is being referred to]? If in the market place, [wearing only a *kaltah*] is a violation of *dat Yehudit*. And if in a [private] courtyard, [if you require a *kaltah* there at all,] you will not leave even one daughter of our forefather Avraham not divorced from her husband!"

If women's *minhag* determines what is *dat Yehudit*, how could R. Zeira challenge R. Asi that "you will not leave even one daughter of our forefather Avraham not divorced"? If all women went bareheaded in their courtyards, then by definition that was the *minhag*, and no violation of *dat Yehudit* was involved!

There are several possibilities:

1. This is proof of the position of *Rosh, Semak* and *Tur* that *dat Yehudit* is not necessarily custom,[83] as explained above. Rather, *dat Yehudit* is a rabbinical enactment like any other. R. Zeira challenged R. Asi that if *dat Yehudit* rabbinically required a woman to wear a *kaltah* in her courtyard, all Jewish women would be in violation.

---

[83] According to all opinions, *dat Yehudit* was not solely a matter of *minhag*. While women could introduce stringencies, only the Sages could decree forfeiture of the *ketubbah*.

2. While *Dat Yehudit* was originally based on custom, it became Halachah and is now unchangeable.[84] R. Zeira challenged R. Asi based on the assumption that originally women had covered their hair in courtyards and that this had become *dat Yehudit,* necessitating the *kaltah* that R. Asi was referring to. Abaye replied that there had never been a custom for women to cover their hair in their own courtyards, and R. Asi was referring to something else.

3. R. Zera's statement, "You will not leave even one daughter of our forefather Avraham undivorced" is clearly hyperbole, as there were many women, such as Kimchit,[85] who did not uncover any hair even inside their homes, let alone in their courtyards. All R. Zeira claimed was that since many women uncover their hair in their courtyards, according to R. Asi's position they would be subject to divorce.

Defining *Kaltah*

Wearing a *kaltah* (lit. "basket"[86]) in public meets the Torah's requirements, but not those of *dat Yehudit*. In the *rishonim* one can ascertain at least four explanations of what is wrong with a *kaltah*:

1. *Quality* of coverage. A *kaltah* was like a woven basket and hair was visible through the interstices (Rivan,[87] *Terumat ha-Deshen*[88]). By contrast, the optimum head covering *(dat Yehudit)* is fully opaque.

---

[84] Similar to R. Zeira's famous statement, "The daughters of Israel initiated the stringency that if a woman sees a drop of blood of even the size of a mustard seed, she counts seven clean days" (*Berachot* 31a). Although originally a *chumra* introduced by women, it became established Halachah.

[85] *Yoma* 47a, "Many [women] acted like Kimchit."

[86] *Bikurim* 3:8, *Ketubbot* 82b, and freq.

[87] Cited in *Shitah Mekubetzet* in *Ketubbot* 72a as "Rashi, first edition."

[88] *Teshuvah* 10.

2. *Quantity.* A *kaltah* was a round cap[89] shaped like a small basket and did not cover all of the woman's hair (R. Yehonatan[90]). *Dat Yehudit* requires that all the hair be covered.

3. *Identity.* A *kaltah* was an actual basket used for carrying small things, carried on top of the head (Rashi,[91] *Nimukei Yosef*[92]). Alternatively, it was a pad or cushion worn on the head to serve as a base for balancing loads (Meiri[93]). In either case, since any girl or woman wore one when she wished to carry things to or from market, it did not identify her as being married,[94] and this violated *dat Yehudit.*

4. *Propriety.* A *kaltah* was a cap used to absorb the grime of the hair, worn under the normal head covering (*Aruch*[95]). It was considered an undergarment and not intended for display, and wearing it in public was a breach of *dat Yehudit.*

I think there is no disagreement between 1 and 2. Both have the same goal of maximum hair coverage: even if the head covering covers the entire head, if hair is visible through the cracks it violates *dat Yehudit,* and even if the covering is opaque but does not cover all the hair it, too, violates *dat Yehudit.* This is in contradiction to Resp. *Igrot Moshe,*[96] who did not consider the possibility that *dat Yehudit* requires covering all of the hair.

---

[89] *Aruch, s.v. klt.*

[90] *Ketubbot* 72a.

[91] *Ibid.*

[92] *Chidushei Nimukei Yosef, ibid.*

[93] *Ibid.*

[94] Covering a woman's hair was a sign of marriage even among the Gentiles, see *Sanhedrin* 58b.

[95] *S.v. kph.*

[96] See below.

What is Rambam's position? *Bach* [97] assumed that Rambam agreed with 1, that a *kaltah*'s disability lay in its porousness, but there appears no indication of this in Rambam. I think that Rambam's view is 4 – that a *kaltah* was a private or informal hair covering that was not considered respectable enough to wear in public even if it covered enough hair. This explains *Hilchot Ishut* 13:11:

> [In] a place where their custom is that a woman does not go out to market with only a cap (*kippah=kaltah*) on her head until she wears a *redid* that covers all of her body like a *tallit*, [her husband] must give her a *redid*....

Why is a *redid* that covers all of her body required for covering her hair? The point is that although a *kaltah* is technically adequate, and in some places wearing one in public is accepted – as is clearly implied by "[In] a place where their custom is...," as noted above[98] – in other places it is not considered respectable for woman to go out in public without a *redid*.

Tefach in Hair

An exposed *tefach* in a woman is *ervah*, and hair in a woman is *ervah*. Does the measurement of a *tefach* also apply to hair? It is not possible to prove anything from the order of the statements in the Gemara.[99]

To Rambam and others,[100] uncovered hair is not an impediment to reciting *Shema* at all. Rather, *se'ar be-ishah ervah* only prohibits pleasurable gazing at any amount of a woman's hair, just as it is forbidden to gaze even at her little finger.

The question of *tefach* or less than *tefach* arises only with *rishonim* who ruled that *se'ar be-ishah ervah* applies to *kriat Shema*. Those *rishonim* who permit *kriat Shema* if less than a *tefach* of flesh is exposed, even in other women,[101]

---

[97] *Orach Chayim* 75.

[98] See above, "Time and Place."

[99] See above, note 1.

[100] See above, note 57.

[101] Especially those who permit up to a *tefach* even in *shok;* see above, "*Shok.*"

are unlikely to be more stringent with hair than with skin. However, those who forbid reciting *kriat Shema* while facing even less than an uncovered handbreadth might hold the same with regard to hair.[102]

Resp. *Igrot Moshe*[103] argued in a different way that a minimum of *tefach* applies also to hair. The Torah requires uncovering the *sotah*'s head[104] (*u-fara et rosh ha-ishah*) and not her hair; therefore, it relates to the hair on the head as a unit and not as individual strands.[105] If the *kohen* uncovered most or at least a large part[106] of her head she was duly considered *pru'at rosh* by Torah law, but certainly not if he uncovered only a small part of it. Since the obligation for a married woman to cover her hair derives from *sotah*, it follows that any woman most of whose hair is covered is not considered by the Torah as *pru'at rosh*. As noted above, R. Feinstein *z"l* overlooked the possibility that *dat Yehudit* required that all the remaining hair also be covered.

He then argued that since the Torah does not designate which part is to be covered, *all* the hair on the head is in the category of a place in the body that is normally covered, and therefore the principle of *tefach be-ishah ervah* applies. But I think this begs the question of whether *tefach* applies to hair in the first place. In addition:

1. Why not argue the opposite? Because no specific part of the hair needs to be covered according to Torah law, none of it is *a priori* in the category of a place normally covered.[107]

2. *Se'ar be-ishah ervah* and *pri'at rosh* stem from two unrelated *sugyot* in *Berachot* and *Ketubbot* respectively. Linking the two is a *chidush*, which requires substantiation.

---

[102] This seems indicated in Ravyah, but the language is not conclusive.

[103] *Even ha-Ezer,* vol. 1, no 58. This is his main *teshuvah* on the topic.

[104] I.e., the part of the head where the hair grows.

[105] The verse cited by R. Sheshet, "Your hair is like a herd of goats," refers to hair in the aggregate.

[106] "*Rov ha-rosh, o le-chol ha-pachot karov le-rov harosh.*" Resp. *Igrot Moshe* does not explain why less than 50 percent would be sufficient.

[107] Particularly if less than 50 percent is sufficient, see previous note.

3. According to Resp. *Igrot Moshe*, a woman's hair is *ervah* only indirectly, by dint of the head being a normally-covered part of the body in accordance with R. Yitzchak's statement. But R. Sheshet's citing the verse from *Shir ha-Shirim* implies that hair is a sexual distraction in its own right.

4. If *u-fara et rosh ha-ishah* determines that all the head is to be considered normally covered and that therefore an uncovered *tefach* of hair is *ervah*, this is a Torah-based determination that cannot be changed whether or not women cover all of their heads in practice. This is similar to the view of *Mishnah Berurah* mentioned above.[108] Yet Resp. *Igrot Moshe* agreed there with *Aruch ha-Shulchan*.[109]

Denying *Igrot Moshe*

In any case, Resp. *Igrot Moshe* permitted uncovering up to a square *tefach* of hair within the hairline. This contradicts *Oz ve-Hadar Levushah*'s portrayal of contemporary Halachah as uniformly forbidding any display of hair. In defense of its position, *Oz ve-Hadar Levushah* claims, first, that Resp. *Igrot Moshe* gave no general *heter* to expose any hair above the forehead:

> People assume that Maran Hagaon Harav Moshe Feinstein *zt"l* allowed women to leave less than a *tefach* uncovered. This is totally incorrect. He allowed this only under pressing circumstances, as is evident from the wording at the beginning of the Responsum.[110]

To buttress his contention, the author then cites a report by a London rabbi of a conversation with R. David Feinstein, in which the latter spoke about his father's ruling:

---

[108] See above, "*Mishnah Beruruah and Aruch ha-Shulchan*."

[109] Resp. *Igrot Moshe, Orach Chayim*, vol. 1, no 42, and see vol. 4, no. 15 (1).

[110] *Oz ve-Hadar Levushah*, p. 236.

Hagaon Rav Dovid *shlita* said to me that it is clear from the text of the *teshuva* that his father *zt"l* never intended to give an all-out *heter* for the exposure of two finger-widths of hair. The *teshuva* was a personal *heter* given for an exceptional case. As he writes, "she [the lady who did not agree to cover her hair] should not be considered a major sinner *ch"v.*" This is also indicated from the introductory words of the *teshuva*, "In the first place I intended not to answer your query in writing, as it is adequate that I give a verbal *heter* when the circumstances justify it" etc. The responsum also finished with the words "It is correct for women to be stringent and cover their hair completely, as the Chassam Sofer held." All this clearly implies that no general *heter* was given.

But Resp. *Igrot Moshe* did not write "she should not be considered a major sinner" in the singular. Instead, he wrote "those [women] who want to be lenient" (*elu ha-rotzot lehakel*) in the plural, referring to women in general, with no mention of any specific "lady who did not agree to cover her hair." Also, Resp. *Igrot Moshe* did not write "she should not be considered a major sinner." Instead, he wrote "they should not be considered violators of *dat Yehudit*" (*ein lehachshivan ke-ovrot al dat Yehudit*), i.e., not sinners at all, neither major nor minor. Thus, he concluded, "even a scholar and a *yarei shamayim* should not refrain from marrying such a woman...."

This pattern of wishful or willful misreading of Resp. *Igrot Moshe* is evident in other points raised. The *teshuvah* was not "a personal *heter* given for an exceptional case." The hesitancy at the beginning of the *teshuvah* refers to replying specifically in writing, not to any hesitancy about the reply itself, and no "pressing circumstances" are involved except as regards writing the *heter* as opposed to transmitting it orally. If there is reluctance to give a "general *heter*" it is in the sense of not circulating it lest it lead women who covered all of their hair until then to lower their standards, but the *heter* was there for anyone who needed it. This explains the remarkable fact that although the *teshuvah* professes to disagree with Resp. *Chatam Sofer*,[111] it makes not the slightest reference to *minhag*, which is a key component of the latter's argument. Resp. *Igrot Moshe* had no intention of prompting women who already had a *minhag le-hachmir* to abandon it.

Oz ve-Hadar Levushah's second argument is that Resp. *Igrot Moshe* retracted his earlier view:

> The ruling mentioned (*O.C.* 4:112) is written in a responsum dated 5717 and again in a responsum (*E.H.* 1:58) dated 5721. There is, however, a third responsum (*O.C.* 4:15) dated 5732 in which it is written explicitly that even less than a *tefach* of hair must be covered in line with other "covered areas" of a woman's body that must be fully covered, and even less than a *tefach* may not be exposed.[112]

This refers to the fact that in the two earlier responsa, *Resp. Igrot Moshe* argued that even *Hagahot Maimoniot* cited by Rema, who forbids viewing less than a *tefach* of flesh in women other than his wife, would permit less than a *tefach* of hair, i.e., that there is no disagreement on this matter. In the third responsum, however, he wrote that the question "depends on the controversy concerning less than a *tefach* [of flesh] brought by Rema," i.e., there *is* disagreement on this matter. According to *Oz ve-Hadar Levushah*, therefore, the last *teshuvah* of Resp. *Igrot Moshe* on the subject rules "explicitly" that any amount of hair must be covered.

However, besides the fact that there is nothing explicit about it, Resp. *Igrot Moshe* did not specify that we rule according to Rema on this issue, but only that it is a matter of controversy. In addition, as opposed to the first two responsa that discuss the Rema/*Hagahot Maimoniot* view, the third responsum has no discussion at all and merely mentions it in passing. It is unlikely that this represents a retraction of his previous arguments.

---

[111] *Orach Chayim*, no. 36.
[112] *Oz ve-Hadar Levushah*, p. 238.

Outside the Hairline

Oz ve-Hadar Levushah does not mention an additional *heter* propounded by Resp. *Igrot Moshe*,[113] that of even more than a *tefach* of hair *outside* the hairline. The source for this leniency is Rashba (and others) in *Berachot* 24a in the name of Ravad:

> Her face, hands and feet, and her speaking voice that is not singing, and her hair outside her *tzamah* that is not covered (*eino mitkaseh*) – they are of no concern (*ein chosheshim lahem*), because he is used to them and they do not distract him.

Hair outside the braided and covered[114] part of her head is mentioned along with her exposed face and feet, which are each more than a *tefach*. But I think this is no proof that Ravad permitted leaving more than a *tefach* of hair uncovered. He was justifying the practice in his time, and the custom then was certainly not for women to expose such quantities of hair inside or outside the hairline. On the contrary, in most if not all medieval communities, married women exposed little or no hair. This is evident from Halachic[115] and pictorial[116] sources.

---

[113] *Even ha-Ezer,* vol. 1, no. 58 (p. 146), and *Orach Chayim,* vol. 4, no. 112 (end).

[114] *U-fara et rosh ha-ishah* has the connotation both of undoing the braids and uncovering the hair; see Resp. *Seridei Eish,* vol. 3, no. 20.

[115] See Resp. *Maharam Alashkar,* no. 35 and *Bnei Banim,* vol. 3, no. 21 (p. 66).

[116] See *Hebrew Illuminated Manuscripts* (Macmillan, 1969), plates no. 8 (from twelfth-century Spain), 10 (fifteenth-century Spain), 22 (thirteenth-century France), 34 (fourteenth-century Germany), 39–40 and 43 (fifteenth-century Germany) and 51 and 54 (fifteenth-century Italy). Most reproductions are also found at random locations in the *Encyclopaedia Judaica*. In a number of the illuminations what appears on women's temples is ornamentation, but their hair is covered just the same. This is as opposed to the third-century murals from the Dura Europus synagogue in Mesopotamia, which portray women's heads as covered but with a band of hair exposed above the forehead and along the sides of the face; see *Encyclopedia Judaica,* vol. 6, columns 283–8 and facing 299–300.

Nevertheless, Resp. *Igrot Moshe* could permit more than a *tefach* outside the hairline simply by following his own line of reasoning. Since the Torah specifies uncovering the *sotah*'s head and not her hair, the *kohen* needed to uncover only the hair on the woman's head, and not what hung down on her neck and shoulders. Consequently, no Torah obligation can be derived for a married woman to cover hair outside her hairline. In the absence of such an obligation, hair outside the hairline would not be considered a place that is normally covered, and *tefach be-ishah* would not apply.

Shoulder-length Hair

However, evidence can be brought from the Gemara that a woman with loose hair down to her shoulders is called *pru'at rosh* even if her head is covered. In *Ketubbot* 15b, the Mishnah states that a maiden goes out to her wedding wearing a *hinuma* and with her head *parua*. Rashi explained that her hair hung down to her shoulders, and in 17a he defined *hinuma* as "a kerchief *(tze'if)* on her head, hanging down over her eyes." Even though she wore a head covering, if her hair fell loose on her shoulders she was deemed *roshah paru'a;* for a married woman to do so would presumably violate *dat Yehudit*.

Separate *Halachot*

Se'ar be-ishah ervah and *dat Moshe ve-Yehudit* stem from two completely separate Talmudic discussions, the first in *Berachot* and the second in *Ketubbot*. The Torah law[117] that married women cover their hair in public, derived in *Ketubbot* from the verse in *Bamidbar,* is independent of the rabbinical laws of *ervah* regarding *kriat Shema* expounded in *Berachot*. Thus, *Aruch ha-Shulchan* wrote:

> For many years daughters of Israel have been wanton in this
> transgression, and they go about bareheaded.... The plague

Plates 55 and 59 from fifteenth-century Italy depict weddings; the first is from a manuscript of *Tur Even ha-Ezer*. Some of the necklines shown would be forbidden according to *Oz ve-Hadar Levushah*.

[117] Or a rabbinic law hinted at in the Torah; see above, note 66.

has spread, and married women go about with their hair [uncovered] like *betulot*. Woe to us that this has happened in our day! However, in any event it seems that, by law, we are permitted to pray and recite blessings facing their uncovered heads, because nowadays most of them go about in this way, and it has become like the normally uncovered parts of her body.[118]

Going bareheaded was and remains a transgression, and only permission for *kriat Shema,* prayers and blessings was effected by widespread violation of the Halachah in this regard. Such violation spread widely in Europe, commencing with the Emancipation in the early nineteenth century. Virtually no Ashkenazic[119] rabbinic authorities justified it.[120]

---

[118] *loc. cit.*

[119] One exception is in *Yad ha-Levi,* a commentary on *Sefer ha-Mitzvot* published in 1926. (Also see Resp. *Sefer Yehoshua,* no. 89.) A handful of Sephardic responders have also done so. I am indebted to Rabbis Aryeh and Dov Frimer for this information. *Ben Ish Chai,* however, in *Halachot* (first collection), *Bo,* par. 12, does not justify the practice but only writes that since women go bareheaded one may recite *Shema* in their presence, similar to *Aruch ha-Shulchan.*

[120] *Shulchan Aruch, Even ha-Ezer* 115, lists *pru'at rosh* under *dat Yehudit* in paragraph 3 but not under *dat Moshe* in paragraph 1. This recently led a colleague to claim that according to *Shulchan Aruch* even going completely bareheaded in public violates only *dat Yehudit,* which is a matter of *minhag* and subject to change. But such a view is (1) impossible according to those who view *pru'at rosh* as a Torah violation, (2) found nowhere in the *rishonim,* and (3) contradicts the *Bet Yosef,* which was written by R. Yosef Karo (the author of the *Shulchan Aruch*).
The problem is that *Shulchan Aruch* combined two incompatible positions. In par. 1 he copied the language of *Tur,* who followed the Mishnah in *Ketubbot* which does not list *pri'at rosh* under *dat Moshe*; see above, "*Dat Moshe and Dat Yehudit*" and in *Bnei Banim,* vol. 3, no. 22. In par. 3, however, *Shulchan Aruch* copied the language of Rambam in *Hilchot Ishut* 24:12 that the source of *dat Yehudit* is *minhag,* which is nowhere mentioned in *Tur.* The two are contradictory, and the intent of *Shulchan Aruch* remains obscure.
However, I think the problem is not in Halachah. Rambam wrote that a woman violates *dat Yehudit* if she goes out to market "*ve-roshah parua ve-ein aleha redid.*" This

Permitted Exposure

By Talmudic law, however, in certain circumstances some exposure of hair was permitted even in the presence of strangers. In *Ketubbot* 72b cited above, "[wearing] a *kaltah* does not constitute [going] bareheaded... [when she goes] from courtyard to courtyard via a passageway (*mavuy*)." As noted above, according to Rivan and *Terumat ha-Deshen* hair was visible through the interstices, and according to R. Yehonatan hair was visible around the *kaltah*[121]; nevertheless, a woman was permitted to wear a *kaltah* in a *mavuy* even though it was a semi-public area and strangers were present.

Semag[122] and R. Yonah[123] wrote that "from courtyard to courtyard via a passageway" means that the woman must go from one to the other without stopping; to tarry she would need optimum hair-covering and not merely a *kaltah*. This may also be the intention of Rivan, who wrote that the hair between the cracks of the *kaltah* is "not so visible" (*ein sa'aroteha nir'in kal kach*) to the men in the passageway. There may have been shops and shopkeepers in the passageway, and if the woman stopped she would be looked at. A glimpse of some of her hair as she walked by, however, was of no consequence. *Nimukei Yosef* even permitted a woman to stop and linger in a *mavuy* while wearing only a *kaltah*, as long as she did not do so regularly *(be-keviut)*.[124]

---

must mean that she is considered *p'ruat rosh* inasmuch as she is not wearing a *redid*, even though she is wearing a *kaltah*. It does not mean that if her head is completely uncovered she violates only *dat Yehudit*, for Rambam wrote in the previous *halachah* that going out completely bareheaded violates *dat Moshe*! Since in par. 3 *Shulchan Aruch* copied Rambam's exact wording, he presumably meant the same thing by it that Rambam did. The difficulty remains that, if so, *Shulchan Aruch* nowhere mentions the prohibition of going out completely bareheaded. That women are forbidden to do so under *dat Moshe*, however, is incontestable.

[121] See above, "Defining *Kaltah*."

[122] *Loc. cit.*

[123] *Loc. cit.*

[124] *Chidushei Nimukei Yosef* to *Ketubbot* 72b. However, he cites Rashi's explanation of *kaltah*, which does not necessarily involve any hair being visible. See above, "Defining *Kaltah*."

In a Courtyard

A woman may go about in a courtyard without any headcovering if no one aside from members of her immediate family sees her there. This is the opinion of Rashi,[125] *Tosafot,*[126] Mahariach,[127] Ran,[128] Ritva[129] and others.[130]

Some *rishonim* seem to have permitted this even when strangers were present. *Nimukei Yosef*[131] wrote:

> In her yard which is not open to many (*she'ein rabim bok'in sham*), she need not be concerned [even] about actual bareheadedness (*pri'at rosh mamash*).

And according to *Terumat ha-Deshen,*[132]

> In a courtyard the woman needs no [head] covering at all… certainly the prohibition of being bareheaded is only because of men's licentiousness (*pritzut de-gavrei*), and where many [men] are not usually found (*lo shechicha rabim*) such as in a courtyard, there is no objection.

The import of both *Nimukei Yosef* and *Terumat ha-Deshen* is that a *kaltah* is mandatory only in a courtyard frequented by many people (*rabim*), but not if only a few visitors are present. One can conceivably discount their wordings as *lav davka* and require a *kaltah* if any stranger is present, as is Ritva's position.[133] But even if so, indubitably, Ritva, *Nimukei Yosef* and *Terumat ha-Deshen* all require in a courtyard *no more* than a *kaltah,* even in the presence of strangers and for an extended period. I think all *rishonim* agree, for this is the

---

125 *Ibid.*

126 *Ibid.*

127 *Hagahot Asheri* in Rosh, *Ketubbot* 7:9.

128 On Rif, *loc. cit.*

129 Comm. to *Ketubbot* 72.

130 This may also be Rambam's position; see *Bnei Banim,* vol 3, no. 21 (p. 65).

131 *Loc. cit.*

132 *Loc. cit.*

133 *Loc. cit.*

sense of "from courtyard to courtyard": the courtyards are, presumably, not both hers, and she cannot assume that no strangers will be there. Nevertheless, a *kaltah* is sufficient even though by many definitions of a *kaltah* some hair is visible.

Moreover, in the Talmud, a courtyard often refers to a central enclosure serving a number of dwellings[134] that are accessible only through the courtyard. I think that Riaz,[135] who wrote, "It is forbidden [for a woman] to go out in a courtyard without a *kaltah* on her head," is referring to such a courtyard and not to a completely private one. He cites the *Yerushalmi* (*Ketubbot* 7:6):

> A woman who goes out in a *kapilton* (=*kaltah*) is not considered as *roshah parua*. This refers to a courtyard, but [if she goes out] to a *mavuy*, she is considered as *roshah parua*.... A courtyard that many people enter (*rabim bok'in bo*) is like a *mavuy*, while a *mavuy* that not many people enter is like a courtyard."

The enclosure under discussion is one that either many people enter or only a few people enter.[136] A completely private courtyard is not under discussion, and the *Yerushalmi* would agree that in the latter case no head covering at all is needed. This is unlike the view that postulates a disagreement between the *Bavli* and *Yerushalmi*.

Similarly, *Tur* wrote in *Even ha-Ezer* 115:

> If she is not wearing a *redid* like all the women [but only a *kaltah*], she is liable to be divorced without [being paid her] *ketubah*, but only if she goes out that way in a public domain, in an open passageway (*mavuy mefulash*) or in a courtyard that many enter. But if [she goes out] in a partially closed

---

[134] As in Mishnah *Eruvin* 2:6, 6:8, and freq.

[135] *Shaltei ha-Giborim* on Rif, *loc. cit.*

[136] "Few people" may also refer to the residents of the houses around the courtyard, as opposed to "many people," i.e., strangers from the outside.

passageway and in a courtyard that few enter, she is not liable to be divorced.

Bach inferred from *Tur* that although the woman is not subject to divorce, it is still improper (*meguneh*) for her to expose any of her hair. But I think that *Tur*, like the *Yerushalmi,* is contrasting a courtyard that many strangers enter with one that few enter but nevertheless some do. In the case of a completely private courtyard, he agrees with Rashi and *Tosafot* that there is no opprobrium in going bareheaded.[137]

Indoors

Talmudic *dat Yehudit* thus establishes a sliding-scale: in one's home or yard when no strangers are present, a woman's hair may be completely uncovered; in a semi-private area where there are a limited number of neighbors or visitors a *kaltah* must be worn, but some hair may remain visible through or outside it without it being considered *pritzut*; while in a frequented area optimum head-covering is required, just as in the marketplace.

However, *Mishnah Berurah*[138] wrote:

> Even if the woman's way is to cover [hair] only in the marketplace but not in [her] house or yard, nevertheless, according to all opinions it is in the category of *ervah* even in the house, and it is forbidden to read *Shema* facing it if [even] part[139] (*miktzat*) of it is uncovered.

According to this ruling, even though the woman may go bareheaded in the privacy of her home without penalty, her husband may not recite *Shema, birkat ha-mazon* or any other blessing or say *divrei Torah* in her presence unless

---

[137] There is no contradiction between this and Kimchit in *Yoma* 47a who was atypical in covering all her hair even indoors, and see *Bnei Banim*, vol 3, no. 21, translated in *RoCJWI*, pp. 137–138.

[138] In 75, sub-par. 10.

[139] According to *Hagahot Maimoniot,* and equating hair with skin.

she covers her hair. In practice, this would make going bareheaded in a family setting impossible, particularly at Shabbat meals.

This would also apply to covered parts of the body, since there is no reason to be more lenient concerning them than concerning hair. Presumably, however, it only applies when these parts of the body are covered for reasons of *tzniut* and not merely for utilitarian reasons. For instance, in cold climates where everyone wears gloves outdoors to keep warm, one would not claim that women's fingers and hands are *ervah* indoors.

However, even with this qualification, the ruling leads to improbable conclusions. In many Arab countries Jewish women went outside with their faces veiled, as already noted in the Mishnah.[140] The veil was for reasons of *tzniut* as defined in those societies. Were the faces of Jewish women, then, considered *ervah* inside their own homes? No one has ever suggested this.

Moreover, what logic is there for ruling that if a woman covers her hair in the marketplace, for example for one hour a day (or week), this alone determines its *ervah* status for all other times and places? This might apply to other women, but not to one's wife, whom he sees all the time at home with her hair uncovered.

Yad Efraim

The source for *Mishnah Berurah*'s ruling is *Yad Efraim,* printed in editions of *Shulchan Aruch Orach Chayim* since 1820. In 75:1, *Shulchan Aruch* wrote that *kriat Shema* is permitted in the presence of virgins who customarily go bareheaded. *Magen Avraham*[141] commented:

> [This is] difficult, for in *Even ha-Ezer* 21:20 [*Shulchan Aruch*] wrote, "Daughters of Israel shall not go bareheaded in the market place, whether married or single," and Rambam also wrote this.

---

[140] *Shabbat* 6:6.
[141] *Orach Chayim* 75, sub par. 3.

Magen Avraham's initial assumption was that the *penuyot* (unmarried women) mentioned in *Even ha-Ezer* are the same as the *betulot* (virgins) mentioned in *Orach Chayim*. On that basis, he pointed to a contradiction: why are *penuyot* forbidden to go bareheaded in the marketplace in *Even ha-Ezer*, while in *Orach Chayim* one is allowed to recite *Shema* in the presence of *betulot* even though they are bareheaded?

Yad Efraim commented on *Magen Avraham*'s difficulty:

> It would seem that it should not be difficult at all, [for we could say that] here [in *Orach Chaim*] where [someone] wants to recite *Shema* in the house or courtyard, there is no prohibition [against doing so in the presence of bareheaded *betulot*, as opposed to in the marketplace]. Perforce [since *Magen Avraham* did find it difficult] one must say that he is of the opinion that, if so, the same would apply even to married women. One is forced to conclude that since married women cover [their hair] in the marketplace, [their hair] is *ervah* regarding *kriat Shema* even indoors.

That is to say: *Magen Avraham* could have resolved the contradiction by explaining that the uncovered hair of *betulot* is *ervah* only in the marketplace, where hair is customarily covered, but not in a house or yard. Since he chose not to do so, it must be because he held that what is *ervah* in public is *ervah* in private, and there is no difference between *betulot* and married women in this regard. Although even if so, it is unclear to me why there should still not be a difference between other married women and one's wife.

Such a *diuk* is a fragile basis for Halachah. It infers from what *Magen Avraham* did not say, and one cannot be sure that that is what *Magen Avraham* meant. Writing after the *Mishnah Berurah*, other compilers[142] ignored this *Yad Efraim*, and its acceptance as Halachah depends on *Mishnah Berurah*'s prestige.[143] In the time of *Yad Efraim* the question was theoretical, since most

---

[142] *Aruch ha-Shulchan, Be'er Yaakov, Caf ha-Chayim*, etc.

[143] Another example of a ruling that achieved prominence only because it was cited by *Mishnah Berurah* is on the question of a woman reading the Megillah for other

women covered their hair both indoors and out. Those who currently cover their hair indoors when in the presence of strangers, but not when alone with their immediate families, have not adopted this *chumrah* in any case.

Resp. *Igrot Moshe*

Disagreeing on logical grounds but without mentioning either *Yad Efraim* or *Mishnah Berurah*, Resp. *Igrot Moshe* wrote in *Yoreh Deah*, part 2, no. 75:

> Concerning a women's hair with regard to her husband when she is a *niddah*, it is certainly better than her normally covered parts. For women who are not stringent like Kimchit but only [observe] what is obligatory and do not cover their hair at home when other men are not present – [the fact] that a woman's husband is continuously familiar with her is a strong argument for not prohibiting it…. In principle it stands to reason that, by law, those covered parts that the husband is forbidden to gaze at are only those parts that are covered at home when only her husband is present, or even when no one at all is present, for women get dressed anyway. It makes no sense [to say] that the covered parts [at home] are those she covers in the marketplace or in the presence of other men when extra *tzniut* is required, although it is good to be stringent in these matters….

Oz ve-Hadar Levushah [144] adopts *Mishnah Berurah*'s view on this matter entirely, and does not mention this Resp. *Igrot Moshe*.[145]

---

women. See my *Equality Lost: Essays in Torah Commentary, Halacha and Jewish Thought* (Urim, 1999), pp. 58–59.

[144] *Oz ve-Hadar Levushah*, 212, 219, 222, 261, etc.

[145] *Sefer Taharat ha-Bayit*, vol. 2, 165 cites Resp. *Igrot Moshe*, but in the digest at the end of the volume (p. 19) the author's son added "on condition that he [her husband] not recite a blessing or *kriat Shema* facing her." This self-contradictory proviso represents *Mishnah Berurah*'s view and not that of *Igrot Moshe*.

C. THE *SUGYOT* IN *KIDDUSHIN* AND *SOTAH*

In *Kiddushin* 70a:

> [R. Nachman said to R. Yehuda,] "Let Donag (R. Nachman's daughter) come and pour us drinks." [R. Yehuda objected:] "Shmuel said, 'One may not make use of a woman.'" [R. Nachman countered: "But] she is a child!" [R. Yehuda replied:] "Shmuel said explicitly, 'One may not make use of a woman at all, whether adult or child.'"

> [R. Nachman then said:] "Would you like to convey greetings (*shalom*) to [my wife,] Yalta?" [R. Yehuda objected:] "Shmuel said, 'A woman's voice is *ervah.*'" [R. Nachman countered:] "It's possible [to send and receive greetings] via an emissary!" [R. Yehuda replied:] "Shmuel said, 'One may not ask about the welfare of a married woman.'" [R. Nachman asked:] "[Not even] via her husband?" [R. Yehuda replied:] "This is what Shmuel said: 'One may not ask about the welfare of a married woman at all.'"

Kol be-Ishah Ervah

In *Berachot* 24a, where Shmuel said, "A woman's voice is *ervah*," it meant her singing voice, as is seen from his citing *Shir ha-Shirim* 2:14, 'Let me hear your voice, for your voice is pleasant (*arev*).'" In *Kiddushin* 70a, however, *kol be-ishah* refers to asking about the welfare (*sh'elah be-shalom*) of a married woman. This has nothing to do with singing. I think his statement there relies on a different Scriptural peg, as found in the Jerusalem Talmud in *Chalah* 2:1:

> Shmuel said, "A woman's voice is *ervah*." What is the reason? "It shall be that from the voice of her whoring (*mi-kol zenutah*), the land will be polluted…." (Jeremiah 3:9)

In context, "voice" here means report or public knowledge, but in its literal connotation it serves as a peg to link women, speech and *zenut*. *She'elat shalom* of a woman, through an emissary or via her husband, relates to *ervah* only in this second sense.[146] Even if transmitted through an intermediary, some words (=voice) can lead to *keruv ha-da'at,*[147] familiarity and affection, and potentially to sin.

Hakol le-Shem Shamayim

As cited by R. Yehuda in *Kiddushin* 70a, Shmuel seems to have prohibited making use of women and *she'elat shalom* of married women in any shape or form. Nevertheless, in *Kiddushin* 81b we find a countervailing principle propounded by none other than Shmuel:

> R. Acha b. Aba visited his son-in-law, R. Chisda. He took his granddaughter on his lap (*otvah be-kanfeih*).... [R. Chisda said to him] "You have violated Shmuel's [prohibition], for Shmuel said, 'One may not make use of a woman.'" [R. Acha b. Aba replied,] "I hold according to Shmuel's other [statement], '*Ha-kol le-shem shamayim* (all in the name of Heaven).'"

---

[146] See *Bnei Banim*, vol. 4, p. 34, note. That Shmuel used *kol be-ishah ervah* in two very different contexts in *Berachot* and *Kiddushin* was noted by *Sefer ha-Makneh* ("*trei mimra de-Shmuel ninhu*") but he did not pursue the matter. Remarkably, this important *Yerushalmi* has been largely overlooked. I have not seen any reference to it in the *Rishonim* other than in Ravyah, chap. 76, *q.v.,* nor in *Acharonim;* even the commentators on the *Yerushalmi* including the recent *Alei Tamar* have no comment *ad loc.*

[147] The common explanation is that making use of women was prohibited because of *hirhur,* as Rambam wrote in *Hilchot Issurei Bi'ah* 21:5. This is also Meiri's view in *Kiddushin* 70a and 81b and what Rashi appears to mean in 82a, and it is implicit in *Tosfot R. Elchanan* quoted below. In *Kiddushin* 70a, however, Rashi explained the issue there as being "lest she learn to frequently be with men." Perhaps the reason is that as opposed to 81b where there was at least an appearance of impropriety (and even more so according to "*Tosfot Ri ha-Zaken,*" who wrote that R. Acha b. Aba took his granddaughter with him to sleep under the bedcovers), it is far-fetched to suppose that if R. Nachman's daughter merely served drinks she would cause *hirhur* in R. Yehuda. Similarly, Rashba in *Berachot* 24b explained the issue of *she'elat shalom* as one of *keruv da'at* and not *hirhur.*

Although one should not make any use of a woman, Shmuel himself permitted reliance on "All in the name (or: for the sake) of Heaven" when circumstances warranted. "In the name of Heaven" in this context means of innocent intent[148] and legitimate purpose, and not necessarily intention to fulfill a specific *mitzvah*.

Rishonim used this principle to justify leniencies that were widespread. *Tosafot* in *Kiddushin*[149] wrote, "We rely on this [*ha-kol le-shem shamayim*] nowadays in that we make use of women," and in *Semag*[150]: "We rely on... 'all [that is] in the name of Heaven.'" In *Berachot* 24a, *Sefer ha-Meorot* wrote in the name of Ravad:

> In another woman, it is certainly forbidden to gaze at any part of her, even at her little finger or her hair, and it is forbidden to hear her words, as is stated in *Kiddushin,* and even *she'elat shalom.* [But] today we are accustomed (*nahigi*) to [permit] *she'elat shalom* and in necessary matters (*u-ve-divrei tzorech*), and [we rely on] *ha-kol le-shem shamayim* as is [mentioned] there.

The references to "we" are to the community in *Tosafot*'s time. The difficulty is that R. Acha b. Aba was a Talmudic sage and presumably on a level far higher than most people. *Tosafot* says as much; in *Shabbat* 13a regarding Ula who kissed his sisters[151] on their hands or sleeves, *Tosafot* wrote:

> He knew that he himself would not come to *hirhur*, as he was a complete *tzaddik (tzaddik gamur)*, as we say in chapter 2 of *Ketubbot* (17a) that R. Ada b. Ahavah[152] used to carry her [the bride] on his shoulders and dance. The [other] rabbis asked

---

[148] "*U-ve-divrei tzorech*" of Ravad, below.

[149] 82a, *s.v. ha-kol le-shem shamayim.*

[150] *Lo Ta'aseh* 126, end.

[151] See my "*Chibuk ve-nishuk krovei mishpachah*" in *Techumin* 21 (5761): 374–384.[*Bnei Banim* vol. 4, no. 13.]

[152] In our editions: R. Acha.

him, "May we do that?"[153] He answered, "If she is like a wooden beam to you, go ahead! Otherwise, no."

And *Tosfot R. Elchanan* wrote in *Avodah Zarah* 17a:

> He [Ula] permitted himself [to do so] because she was like a wooden beam to him, as is said in chapter 2 of *Ketubbot* regarding a bride. And it is said in *Kiddushin,* "I hold like Shmuel's other [statement], '*Ha-kol le-shem shamayim.*'"

R. Acha b. Aba is thus equated with Ula and R. Acha, who were complete *tzaddikim* and to whom women were like "wooden beams." But if so, how could *Tosafot, Semag* and Ravad extrapolate from him to people in their day? The ability of a *tzaddik gamur* to refrain from *hirhur* says nothing about lesser mortals!

There are a number of possibilities:

1. R. Acha b. Aba was indeed a *tzaddik gamur,* but that is not the reason he gave. Since his justification was *ha-kol le-shem shamayim* and not that this woman was like a "wooden beam" to him, one learns from this that *le-shem shamayim* is sufficient even if one is not a *tzaddik.*

2. Only in extreme cases need one be a *tzaddik gamur.* Thus R. Acha, who carried a bride on his shoulders, explained that she was like a "wooden beam" to him, and R. Gidel who in *Berachot* 20a sat at the entrance to a women's *mikveh (sha'arei tevilah),* explained that they were like "white geese," because otherwise it would have been impossible to avoid *hirhur* in such circumstances. In less provocative situations, however, even the average person can claim *ha-kol le-shem shamayim.*

---

[153] Perhaps this took place at a wedding or *sheva berachot* attended only by rabbis and scholars but not common people, who would not have known what to make of it. With that, there are hints that dancing arrangements at weddings then were different from what they are today; see *Nedarim* 51a and *Bnei Banim,* vol. 1, no. 37 (3).

3. As an individual, only a complete *tzaddik* like R. Acha b. Aba may take liberties in matters of *hirhur*. But the community as a whole has a different status, and therefore *Tosafot* wrote that "we" can and do make use of women. The reason is that the everyday, routine and commonplace nature of a practice forestalls *hirhur*.[154]

Special Leniencies

Rishonim differ as to whether egregious behavior such as R. Gidel's sitting near the entrance to the women's mikveh and R. Acha's dancng with a bride on his shoulders can be permitted at all in later generations. Nowadays, may even a saint do what they did? *Sefer ha-Chinuch*[155] answered no, and moreover made no distinction between radical cases such as those of R. Gidel and Rav Acha and everyday circumstances:

> In everything that they *z"l* warned us, a man is not permitted to deviate from their good counsel.... That you find a few incidents in the Gemara which appear to contradict my words is no contradiction at all. Only in a case of a *mitzvah* were they slightly lenient, as we find that R. Yochanan[156] used to sit at *sha'arei tevilah* so that the women would look at him and give birth to children as good-looking as he was, and he never looked at them, *chalilah*. And Rabi,[157] who put a bride on his shoulders, did so for a *mitzvah*, to cause her joy.... Also they *z"l* were like angels, who did not occupy themselves even momentarily with anything but Torah and *mitzvot*... and they felt no wicked feeling in anything.... But

---

[154] See my article "The Significant Role of Habituation in Halakhah," in *Tradition*, Fall 2000 [reprinted below], and further remarks in the Spring 2001 issue.

[155] *Mitzvah* 188.

[156] In our editions R. Yochanan also sat near *sha'arei tevilah*, but it is R. Gidel who remarked that women are like "white geese."

[157] In our editions, R. Acha.

we, today, are not to make even the slightest breach in these matters.

Semak,[158] however, wrote that someone to whom women are like geese or a wooden beam is permitted to look at them, and did not limit this to Talmudic times. Similarly, Meiri wrote in *Ketubbot*[159] that only someone free of all *hirhur* can carry a bride on his shoulders or gaze at her in order to endear her to the groom, the implication being that there are such individuals even today. In *Kiddushin*[160] Meiri wrote that one is permitted *she'elat shalom* of a married woman (only) if he has no trace (*srach*) of *hirhur*, "and on this and the like it is said '…and you shall fear your G-d; I am *ha-Shem*,'" i.e., a person is permitted to claim that he has no *hirhur*, and G-d will judge whether he is being truthful.[161]

Ritva[162] wrote:

> Everything depends on what a person recognizes in himself. If he recognizes that his impulses are overcome and under his control and he has no lust at all, he is permitted to look at and speak with an *ervah* and inquire about a married woman's welfare. Such is the case of R. Yochanan who sat at the gates of [the place of women's] immersion and was not afraid of the evil inclination… and R. Ada b. Ahavah,[163] about whom it is said in *Ketubbot* that he placed a bride on his shoulders and danced with her, and was not afraid of *hirhur* for the reason mentioned. However, it is not proper (*ein ra'uy*) to be lenient in this, other than a great *chasid* who knows his impulses (*yitzro*), and not all scholars [can] rely on their impulses [being under control].

---

[158] *Mitzvah* 30.

[159] 17a.

[160] 70a.

[161] Cf. the variant in mss. of Ritva, *"ha-kol le-fi da'at shamayim."*

[162] End of *Kiddushin.*

[163] In our editions, R. Acha.

In theory, extraordinary individuals can take liberties that are forbidden to others. But in practice, who can claim to have reached such a level? Moreover, Ritva equates looking at, speaking to and inquiring about an *ervah* with the more extreme cases of R. Acha and R. Gidel or R. Yochanan. For any leniency, then, one needs to be a *chasid gadol*.[164]

Individuals and Community Norms

The above would seem to be in clear disagreement with *Tosafot, Semag, Sefer ha-Meorot* and Ravad, none of whom stipulated any condition about being extraordinary individuals. But I think there is disagreement only according to the first two suggestions of how and what *Tosafot* learned from R. Acha b. Aba, listed above. According to the third, there is no *machloket*. *Semak,* Meiri and Ritva deal with individuals, but *Tosafot, Semag* and Ravad refer to whole communities whose practices have changed: "*We* rely on [*ha-kol le-shem shamayim*] nowadays in that we make use of women"; "Today, *we* are accustomed to *she'elat shalom* and in necessary matters, and *ha-kol le-shem shamayim*." An individual cannot interact with women more than do his peers without exposing himself to *hirhur*. But if such is everyone's day-to-day behavior, it loses its provocative character.

Leket Yosher

The author of *Terumat ha-Deshen* is quoted in *Leket Yosher*[165]:

> He said that it is permitted to walk behind the wife of a
> *chaver* or behind his mother, because nowadays we are not all

---

[164] An exception to this is R. Yonah in *Berachot* in the name of R. Hai Gaon, who wrote, "Even when she is playing (=singing), if he can concentrate on his prayers so that he doesn't listen and doesn't pay attention to her, it is permitted and he should not interrupt his prayers. Similarly, when she exposes a *tefach* it is not forbidden [to pray] except while gazing at her, but simply seeing her is permitted." This refers to anyone and not just a *chasid gadol*. However, the language "he should not interrupt his prayers" suggests *bedieved*: if he was praying and a woman began singing he need not stop, but if she was already singing he should not start.

[165] *Yoreh Deah*, p. 37.

that prohibited (*ein anu muzharim kol kach*) from walking behind a woman.

Walking behind a woman is explicitly prohibited in *Berachot* 61a because of *hirhur*,[166] and just who permitted it? However, because nowadays women go everywhere and we are accustomed to walking in back of them, no *hirhur* results.[167]

Maharshal

In *Yam shel Shlomoh*[168] Maharshal quoted both *Tosafot* and Ritva, and he wrote in the introduction[169]:

> It will be explained that everything is according to what his eyes see, and [if he] controls his impulses and can overcome them he is permitted to speak to and look at an *ervah* and inquire about her welfare. The whole world (*kol ha-olam*) relies on this in using the services of and speaking to and looking at women; nevertheless, it is forbidden for maidservants to attend to him in the bath[house].

The first sentence mirrors Ritva, while the second restates *Tosafot* and makes explicit what was implicit:

1. *Tosafot* is referring to the whole community (*kol ha-olam*) and not just to themselves. Simple people as well as scholars rely on *ha-kol le-shem shamayim*.

---

[166] Rivevan in *Berachot* and Resp. *Radbaz*, part. 2. no. 770; and see below, "Ideology." Rashi gives a different reason, that it is dishonorable (*genai*) to walk behind a woman, but this does not fit into the language of *Leket Yosher*.

[167] See Resp. *Tzitz Eliezer* vol. 9, no. 50; Resp. *Yabia Omer*, vol. 6, *Orach Chayim*, no. 13 (5); and my article in *Tradition*, Fall 2000, note 23 and remarks in Spring 2001. See above, note 154 (and *Bnei Banim*, vol. 4, no. 13[7]).

[168] *Kiddushin* 4:25.

[169] On the introductions in *Yam shel Shlomoh*, see *Bnei Banim* vol. 1, p. 35, note, and vol. 2, p. 233.

2. *Tosafot* cited "to make use of women" only as an example. The leniency equally applies to looking at and speaking to women, etc. – whatever is normal in day-to-day affairs.

3. *Tosafot* did not permit activities that inherently lead to *hirhur,* such as being washed by maidservants. This is an extreme case and would require one to be a *chasid gadol,* as would carrying a bride on one's shoulders.

Levush

R. Mordechai Yafeh, who studied under Maharshal, openly subscribes to the third possibility listed above as to how *Tosafot* learned from R. Acha b. Ada. In the *Minhagim* at the end of his *Levush Orach Chayim* he wrote, regarding mixed seating[170] at wedding feasts:

> Nowadays we are not careful about [avoiding] this, possibly because nowadays women are very common among men, and there is not so much[171] sinful *hirhur* [about them], because they seem to us like "white geese" due to the frequency of their being among us. And what [people] got used to, they paid no attention to (*kayvan de-dashu, dashu*[172]).

Embodiments of this approach in recent times were the strictly Orthodox Germanic-Dutch Jewish communities,[173] largely destroyed in World War II but of which remnants have survived in different countries. They were characterized by mixed men-and-women seating at weddings, social events and even *shiurim,* by handshakes between men and women, etc. – *ha-kol le-shem shamayim.*

---

[170] See *Bnei Banim*, vol. 1 no. 35, translated in *RoCJWI*, chap. 19, and see *Otzar ha-Poskim*, vol. 17, p. 107.

[171] *Hirhur averah* is one of three things no man escapes daily, *Bava Batra* 164b.

[172] See *Gittin* 56b.

[173] Despite attempts in some circles to doctor history.

Levush's concluding statement, *kayvan de-dashu, dashu,* can also mean "what was done, was done,"[174] i.e., it might have been preferable had women's presence not become commonplace among men, but since it has, we judge matters accordingly. This is similar to *Aruch ha-Shulchan*'s observation on the consequences of women going bareheaded.[175] But there is an important difference: the requirement for married women to cover their heads in public is of Torah origin and cannot change, and is independent of *hirhur.* Therefore, Halachah continues to insist that women cover their hair. By contrast, the strictures against interaction with women are meant to forestall *hirhur* and related hazards. If these are ameliorated by "the frequency of their being among us," as *Levush* wrote, there is no obligation to return to conventions that prevailed in the time of the Talmud. From *Tosafot* through *Levush,* we find no exhortation to turn the clock back to more pristine times.

Christian and Muslim Societies

Tosafot[176] reflect the changed role of women in their time. For example, in *Avodah Zarah* 23a, on the question of whether seclusion (*yichud*) with a non-Jew results in a woman being forbidden to her *kohen* husband, *Tosafot* wrote:

> If so, you will not have even one daughter of our forefather Abraham[177] who is the wife of a *Kohen* left married to her husband, for it is impossible that she will never be secluded with any non-Jew at least for a brief interval (*sha'ah achat*).

This reflected conditions in Christian France, where in the Jewish community wives often ran the family businesses when their husbands were away. Extensive contact with non-Jews was involved, and inadvertent *yichud* at one time or another was almost inevitable. One cannot imagine, say,

---

[174] Cf. *Bereishit* 43:14; Esther 4:16.

[175] See above, "*Mishnah Brerurah and Aruch ha-Shulchan.*"

[176] *S.v. Ve-to.*

[177] The idiom is from *Ketubbot* 72b; see above, "The *sugya* in *Ketubbot.*"

Rambam[178] using such an argument, for in Muslim societies women played no such role and were heavily chaperoned.

Distinctions in *Kol be-Ishah*

Various arguments and considerations have been advanced and gradations have been proposed regarding *kol be-ishah*:

1. Singing that is recorded, broadcast or electronically amplified (heard only through a loudspeaker), is preferable to live performance. A voice converted into electrical impulses and then reconverted into audible sound is technically not a "voice."

2. Two or more women singing together are preferable to a soloist, because of the difficulty of hearing any one voice clearly.[179]

3. Singing along with the women by the man or men is preferable to passive listening.[180]

4. A situation where the singer is not visible[181] is preferable to one where she is.

5. A situation where the singer is not known to the listener is preferable to one where she is.[182]

---

[178] Cf. Rambam, *Hilchot Ishut* 13:11 on a husband not permitting his wife to go out more than "once or twice a month," and see *Bnei Banim*, vol. 1, no. 40, translated in *RoCJWI*, chap. 24.

[179] *"Trei kolei lo mishtam'ei,"* see *Rosh ha-Shanah* 27b.

[180] *Tosafot Sotah* 39b, *s.v. Ad she-yichleh,* "When they themselves sing, they do not hear the voices of their friends." The circumstances there are of men singing together; however, there is no reason to distinguish them from men and women singing together on account of the distinct vocal tones of men and women, for men are themselves divided into basses, baritones, tenors and countertenors.

[181] See Ravyah, below.

[182] See below.

6. *Zemirot Shabbat*[183] and songs using verses from *Tanach* or the *siddur,* etc. sung for religious reasons, are preferable to secular songs. Not to compare, Israeli folk songs are preferable to popular music, etc.

Choral Singing

In *Sotah* 48a:

> R. Yosef said, "When men sing (*zamri*) and women respond ('*ani*), it is *pritzuta;* when women sing and men respond it is like fire in kindling." What difference does it make [how we describe them]? To determine what should be abolished first.

Rashi explained:

> "Like fire in kindling" – because one who responds inclines his ear to hear the singer, [to be able] to respond after him. The result is that the men pay close attention (*notnim libam*) to the women's voice[s], and [since] *kol be-ishah* is *ervah,* as it is written (*Shir ha-Shirim* 2:14) "Let me hear your voice," it inflames his *yetzer* like fire in kindling. But when men sing and women respond, [although] there is a little immodesty (*ketzat pritzut*) because of *kol be-ishah ervah,* it does not inflame his *yetzer* so much, because the singers do not incline their ears [to listen carefully] to the voice[s] of the responders.

Rashi means that for men to respond as a chorus to what the women sing,[184] they need to listen attentively to the women. Attentiveness nullifies the effect of *trei kali,*[185] and therefore the women's voices inflame the men's *yetzer ha-ra*. When men lead and women respond, however, the men do not

---

[183] *Sefer Divrei Chefetz,* cited in *Sdei Chemed, Ma'arechet "Kuf,"* no. 42.
[184] Cf. Mishnah *Sotah* 5:4 and *Sukkah* 38b.
[185] See *Megillah* 21a, *Rosh ha-Shanah* 27a.

have to listen attentively – although of course they hear the women singing – and therefore there is only a "little" *pritzut*.

According to this, if men listen without special concentration, *trei kali* does not completely obviate *kol be-ishah* but it minimizes it. This raises the possibility that if the men are not listening at all or, alternatively, they themselves sing along or there are other mitigating factors along with *trei kali*, the result would be that there is no *pritzut* altogether. The fact that the Gemara does not state a greater *chidush* – that there is *pritzut* even when men and women sing in unison rather than responsively – is an indication of this.

Rashi in *Sotah* further cited *Shir ha-Shirim* 2:14, "let me hear your voice" (*hashmi'ini et kolech*). The verse continues "for your voice is pleasant," which is the Scriptural peg for *kol be-ishah ervah* cited in *Berachot* 24a. This is the prototypical *kol be-ishah*[186]: a single woman singing for a man who enjoys listening to her.

Visibility

There are differing views on the connection between *kol be-ishah ervah* and a woman's being visible:

1. A woman's singing voice is *ervah* even when she is not visible. (*Sefer Yere'im*,[187] *Mordechai*[188])

2. A woman's singing voice is *ervah* only when she *is* visible. (Ravyah[189])

3. *Kol be-ishah* is *ervah* if the listener has previously seen the woman, even if she is not now visible while singing. (*Acharonim*[190])

---

[186] For refutation of a recent claim that *kol be-ishah* is *not* a general proposition as to the sexually arousing nature of a woman's voice, see my *Equality Lost*, chap. 8.

[187] *Loc. cit.* See above, note 38.

[188] *Berachot, loc. cit.*

[189] *loc. cit.*

[190] See Resp. *Yabia Omer*, vol. 1, *Orach Chayim*, no. 6 (11).

The first view, that she need not be visible at all, is implicit in *Sefer Yere'im*:

> It is forbidden to recite *kriat Shema* or a *davar she-bi-kedushah* while hearing a woman's voice in song. [But] because of our sins, we dwell among the nations, and "it is a time to act for *ha-Shem*, violate the Torah" – therefore, we are not careful not to learn while hearing the voices of Gentile women.

In crowded urban conditions it was impossible to escape the sound of non-Jewish women singing. Obviously, the Gentile women were not inside the *bet midrash*. Their voices were heard from adjacent houses and courtyards, and there is no reason to assume that the Jews necessarily saw them or knew who was singing. Nevertheless, if not for "it is a time to act for *ha-Shem*," it would have been forbidden to learn Torah because of *kol be-ishah ervah*.

Kol in a Woman

The second view is found in Ravyah, who wrote as a second explanation: "Some explain [that *kol be-ishah* is *ervah*] because a man usually looks at her when she sings." This fits the language *kol be-ishah*, literally a voice "in a woman" and not disembodied "of a woman." In the same way that *se'ar be-ishah* refers only to hair attached to the body and not after its having been cut, even if worn as a wig,[191] *kol be-ishah* refers to a voice "attached" to a woman. This is hinted at in *Shir ha-Shirim*, "for your voice is pleasant and your appearance is attractive," which links hearing and seeing.

In *Sotah* 8a, the Gemara states, "We have learned that [a man's] evil inclination rules only in what (*be-mah*) his eyes see," which also supports Ravyah's view. But it is not proof, for the statement can be understood in several ways:

1. Sense perception is essential for the *yetzer hara* to rule. "What his eyes see" is a prime example, but the same applies to

---

[191] Rema in 85:2.

hearing, touch, etc. As the Sages said,[192] "Can't a blind person perform all the abominations in the world?"

2. That a man's evil inclination "rules" *(sholet)* in what his eyes see means that vision is the main cause of *hirhur*. However, it is not the only catalyst; hearing can also cause *hirhur*, albeit less so than sight. A man may overhear the sultry song of a woman he does not know and fantasize that she is a temptress, only to discover upon meeting her that she is ugly and no object of desire.[193]

Seeing and Recognition

The third view is that if one knows a woman her singing is *ervah* to him even if she is not now visible, but not otherwise. As *Tosafot* wrote in *Sotah* 8a:

> [People] raise a question from *Chagigah* (11b), "Regarding forbidden relations *(arayot)*, his [evil] inclination waxes whether [they are] before him or not." [But] that is no difficulty, for what it means is that someone who saw an *ervah* once always has *hirhurim* about her.

Similarly, the Gemara in *Megillah*[194] declares that anyone who exclaimed "Rachav, Rachav!" had an immediate seminal discharge. *Tosafot* in *Sanhedrin* 45a asked how this could be reconciled with the statement that the *yetzer ha-ra* rules only in what the eyes see. It answered that the Gemara itself explains that such a discharge occurred only in the case of someone familiar with her *(bi-yod'ah u-ve-makirah)*. Ergo, if one knows a woman, she can be the cause of *hirhur* whether she is present and visible or not.

However, I think this is not conclusive with regard to *kol be-ishah*. If the *yetzer ha-ra* reacts more strongly to seeing than to hearing, as suggested above, one cannot extrapolate from the former to the latter. It is also unclear

---

192 *Sifrei Bamidbar* 116.
193 *Biyod'ah u-ve-makirah* works both ways; see below, "Seeing and recognition."
194 15a, and *Ta'anit* 5b.

what can be learned from Rachav and the other women mentioned there in *Megillah*. According to the *gemara* they were the most beautiful women in history, and what applied to them may not apply to others.[195]

Pictures

Is seeing a picture or a photograph of a woman the same as *yod'ah u-makirah*? Some cite *Sanhedrin* 39b as proof that pictures can arouse, and therefore that all photographs of women are to be avoided:

> Achav was a repressed (*metzunan*) individual, and Izevel made two images (*tzurot*) of prostitutes for his chariot, so that he would see them and become aroused.

But what were these "images of prostitutes"? Either they portrayed prostitutes whom Achav knew and would recognize as such, or they were erotic pictures of anonymous women who for that reason were deemed *zonot*. If the first, it does not prove that pictures have any effect unless the woman is known to be a *prutzah*. If the second, it does not demonstrate that pictures of ordinary women cause *hirhur,* but only that pornography, obviously, does.

D.   PRINCIPLES OF *PESAK*

Lo Plug

In general, *lo plug* (a characteristic of rabbinic legislation not to allow for exceptions) does not apply in matters of *hirhur.* If it did, R. Acha would not have lifted a bride on his shoulders and R. Gidel and R. Yochanan would not have sat at the entrance to a women's *mikveh*, etc., nor could *Semak,*

---

[195] In particular, Rachav had been a prostitute, as recorded in Joshua 2:1, and see *Zevachim* 116b and *Sifrei Bamidbar* 10. This accounts for the two verbs "*bi-yod'ah u-ve-makirah,*" i.e., one who had both seen how beautiful she was and knew her professionally; cf. Maharsha and *Iyun Yaakov* in *Ta'anit* 5b.

Ritva and Meiri have permitted special individuals to exempt themselves from many of the strictures regarding *hirhur,* even today.[196]

Even Resp. *Radbaz,*[197] who wrote that regarding the prohibition of walking behind a woman all women in all countries are the same, did not write that all men are the same. This distinction between who is subject to the enactment (men) and what or whom the enactment is about (women), with only the latter being subject to *lo plug,* is made by *Taz* and cited by *Biur Halachah* in *Orach Chayim* 275:1.

Vox Populi

Widespread practices influence rabbinic rulings in a number of ways. Some examples are:

1. "Go see what the people say"[198] (*puk chazi mai ama davar*). In case of doubt as to what is halachah, custom is decisive in choosing between various options.

2. "Better that they be unwitting violators than deliberate ones"[199] (*mutav she-yiheyu shogegin ve-al yiheyu mezidin*). An anti-halachic custom that is firmly entrenched and unlikely to be changed should not be openly challenged.[200]

---

[196] This applies to *hirhur* but not necessarily to *kriat Shema,* i.e., a saint may permit himself to look at what is rabbinically *ervah,* but he would still be forbidden to recite *kriat Shema* facing it, *lo plug* devolving on the latter but not on the former. Only R. Hai Gaon, as cited by R. Yonah, clearly permits both. On the underlying issue of whether *tefach be-ishah,* etc., as regards *kriat Shema* is a question of *hirhur* or an independent rabbinical decree, see especially *Sefer Bnei Tzion* (Lichtman) on *Orach Chayim* (vol. 2), sect. 75, nos. 1–4 at length, and in Resp. *Mishneh Halachot,* vol. 7, no. 13.

[197] Part 2, no. 770.

[198] *Berachot* 48b.

[199] *Beitzah* 30a.

[200] On who and what is included in *mutav she-yiheyu shogegin,* see *Bnei Banim,* vol. 2, no. 27. On reconciling *mutav she-yiheyu shogegin* with the Torah commandment of rebuke (*tochechah*), see vol. 3, *maamar* 1.

3. When a practice seemingly violates Halachah, it may prompt (re)examination of the sources in an effort to discover grounds for it[201] *(limmud zechut).* If they are strong enough, these grounds may legitimize the practice.

What may be *puk chazi* in the opinion of one *posek* may be *mutav she-yiheyu shogegin* in the eyes of another. This is particularly the case in matters of *tzniut,* where subjectivity is intrinsic.

Reality

In general, Halachah – pristine, theoretical law as derived from the sources – is blended with factors "on the ground" – such as *le-chatchilah* and *bedieved, mutav she-yiheyu shogegin,* extenuating circumstances *(sha'at ha-de-chak),* etc. – to produce *hora'ah,* an actual ruling. Often, familiarity with reality and an intuitive grasp of what is possible and needed in a given community distinguishes a *posek* from one who is merely a great Torah scholar.

A grasp of reality plays another role as well. Preliminary evaluation of a situation may determine the Halachic arguments brought to bear on it. My grandfather[202] and teacher, the *gaon* and *posek, ztz"l,* wrote on the topic of *agunah,* a woman whose husband is missing and presumed dead:

---

[201] *Limmud zechut* usually involves the following elements: (1) an established or intractable practice (2) seemingly at variance with Halachah, which is (3) practiced by essentially Torah-observant communities and for which (4) grounds or support can indeed be adduced or found, even if normally we would rule otherwise. Determining when these conditions are met is the responsibility of *poskim* on the scene. They can be met in the case of increased mingling of the sexes, as I illustrated with the case of the Germanic-Dutch *Yekkishe* communities.

[202] R. Yosef Eliyahu Henkin (1881–1973) was born in White Russia and immigrated to the United States in 1924. For years before and after World War II he was the preeminent Halachic authority in America. He was also widely revered as a *tzaddik,* partly because of decades of selfless devotion to the Ezras Torah charity fund he directed. For a biography see my *Equality Lost,* chap. 16, and see *Encyclopaedia Judaica,* 1974 Yearbook, p. 415. [See, also, *Bnei Banim* vol. 4, *maamar* 1.]

It is known that the *gedolim* first evaluated the situation, and [only] after it was clear in their minds that he [the husband] was indeed dead, they spliced together [*tzarfu*] various Halachic arguments [to that effect].[203]

Similarly, in matters of *tzniut*, if I am certain there is *hirhur* I will be unmoved by considerations such as whether a voice heard over the radio is technically a woman's voice or not. If, on the other hand, I perceive there is no *hirhur*, I will be more receptive to countervailing arguments.

Limits to Enactments

A man may not gaze at the colored clothes of a woman he knows lest he bring himself to *hirhur*.[204] In *Bereishit* 49:11, Rashi explained the verse *kibes ba-yayin levusho u-ve-dam anavim suto:*

> Colored [clothes], from the word *sutah*, "to incite." The woman wears them in order to entice the male (*mesitah ba-hen et ha-zachar*) to look at her.

That being the case, why didn't the Sages forbid the wearing of colored clothes altogether, at least outside the home? I think they were unable to and unwilling to. Women seek to be attractive and would not accept such a prohibition, any more than they would agree not to wear jewelry on *Shabbat* because of the dangers of carrying.[205]

This accords with the explanation of Rashi and of most *rishonim* of *dat Yehudit*[206] as customs that modest women first accepted on themselves. The Sages could not impose everything unilaterally.[207]

---

[203] *Lev Ivra*, p. 29, in *Kitvei haGri"a Henkin*, vol. 1, p. 164. Also in *Otzar ha-Poskim*, vol. 4 (5717), p. 354.

[204] *Avodah Zarah* 21a; *Shulchan Aruch, Even ha-Ezer* 21:1.

[205] *Shulchan Aruch, Orach Chayim* 303:18. In the case of colored clothes it is the responsibility of the man not to look, and not the responsibility of the woman to avoid affording the man something to look at. See *Bnei Banim*, vol. 3, no. 26 (2–3).

[206] See above, *"Dat Moshe and Dat Yehudit."*

Ideology

Books such as *Oz ve-Hadar Levushah* are as much about ideology and outlook as they are about Halachah. This ideology prohibits a woman from standing out and from being outstanding. She must not act in a play, paint a mural, play an instrument or otherwise demonstrate special skills in front of men, lest she attract attention and her movements excite them.[208]

But I think no such *issur* exists. For example, *Oz ve-Hadar Levushah's* source for the above is the Resp. *Radbaz* previously cited[209]:

> The basic reason [for not walking behind a woman] is that because of her walking and movements (*hiluchah utenu'ateha*) he will arrive at *hirhur,* even if she is fully covered... he is forbidden to walk even in back of his wife.... If she is far enough away so that he does not recognize and discern her walking and her movements, it is permitted, but [in] any [circumstances in which] he sees and discerns her walking and the movements of her limbs, it is prohibited.

From this, Resp. *Mishneh Halachot*[210] adduced that watching *any* movement of a woman's limbs is prohibited, even if clothed. But clearly, according to Radbaz, "her walk and her movements" refers to the distinctively feminine sway of the hips and body while walking.[211] It has nothing necessarily to do with movements that are identical in both men and

---

[207] Cf. the recurrent and often futile attempts to prevent the use by *Haredi* women of natural-looking or otherwise eye-catching wigs (sheitels), see *Oz ve-Hadar Levushah,* pp. 245–254. R. Falk subsequently published a 42-page English booklet plus sources in Hebrew, entitled "A Halachic Guide to Present-Day Sheitels." This coincided with the reposting in neighborhoods in Jerusalem of wall-posters from a decade earlier forbidding the use of such wigs.

[208] *Oz ve-Hadar Levushah,* p. 470.

[209] See above, *"Lo Plug."*

[210] Vol. 6, no. 25.

[211] Cf. *Avodah Zarah* 18a, *"dikdekah be-fsi'oteha."*

women and have no sensuous aspect to them, such as playing the piano, playing a violin or peeling a potato.

I have no quarrel with Resp. *Mishneh Halachot*, who is entitled to his opinion. I do have a quarrel with popularizers such as *Oz ve-Hadar Levushah*, who copy such opinions as if they were basic Halachah.[212]

Excellence in *Tzniut*

According to this ideology, the one area in which a woman should strive to excel is that of *tzniut* itself. Just as a man has the study of Torah, a woman has the practice of *tzniut*.[213] The world of *tzniut* is all-encompassing,[214] and women are expected to "work on their *tzniut*" as a counterpoint to the man's day-and-night Torah study.[215] A woman's ultimate distinction is to be considered a *tzenuah*.[216]

Oz ve-Hadar Levushah mentions, approvingly,

> ...a *rebbetzin* who never displayed her vast knowledge. Whenever the words of the Rambam, the *Chovas Levavos* or the *Mesilas Yesharim* were quoted at the Shabbas table or at a family gathering, she would listen quietly and closely as if the words were new. She never hinted that she was fully acquainted with what was being quoted.[217]

An alternative – that she should share her knowledge with others and deliver a *devar Torah* – is not considered. Apparently, that would be displaying special skills and reflect a lack of *tzniut*. The author does not raise the issue of women's Torah learning directly, but it is clear that he does not expect women to challenge or be challenged intellectually.

---

[212] For another example of this, the supposed prohibition of carrying the groom on one's shoulders at a wedding, see *Bnei Banim*, vol. 1, no. 37 (13).

[213] *Oz ve-Hadar Levushah*, p. 40.

[214] Ibid., p. 37.

[215] Ibid., p. 42, in the name of *Chazon Ish*.

[216] Ibid., p. 38.

[217] Ibid., p. 45.

In a sense, books like *Oz ve-Hadar Levushah* continue the process of standardization of Halachah at the expense of local custom, which began with *Mishnah Berurah* and has continued in earnest since the European Holocaust. *Tzniut* is particularly ill-suited for such standardization, and what is suitable for *kiddush*-cups and *matzot* may not be suitable for the amount of a woman's hair showing, if any. There is a danger here of losing sight of the real basics of modesty — not to mention being so concerned about not thinking about women that one can think of nothing else.

CHAPTER TWO

THE SIGNIFICANT ROLE
OF HABITUATION IN HALACHAH

ONE OF THE OFFSHOOTS of the contemporary preoccupation with sex is the tendency to read sexual considerations into *halachot* where they don't belong. Two examples come readily to mind. Rabbi Moshe Meiselman, in his book *Jewish Woman in Jewish Law*,[1] explains the *beraita* in *Megillah* 23a, "…but the Sages said, a woman may not read the Torah because of *kevod ha-tzibbur*," as referring to the probability that a woman reader would arouse impure thoughts in listening males. He offers no source for such a contention, which is almost certainly in error, as none of the other Talmudic references to *kevod tzibbur* has the slightest sexual context.[2] Rather, as *Petach ha-Devir* explains, *kevod ha-tzibbur* regarding women's Torah readings refers to the damage to a community's good name caused by relying on the services of women readers, for this gives the impression that there are not enough men competent to read themselves.[3]

---

[1] p. 142.
[2] See *Yoma* 70a, *Megillah* 23b, *Gittin* 60a, and *Sotah* 39b.
[3] *Petach ha-Devir* 282:9. For this reason R. Yaakov Emden, in his *Hagahot* to *Megillah* 23a, writes that women may be called to read if in fact there are not enough men

Among the *rishonim, Sefer ha-Meorot* is explicit that *kevod ha-tzibbur* as regards women's *aliyot* does *not* mean sexual distraction: "That which we say, 'A woman may not read the Torah because of *kevod ha-tzibbur*' – the reason is *kevod ha-tzibbur*, but there is no *pritzuta* (licentiousness)."[4] Furthermore, Maharam Rottenberg rules that in a town where all the males are *kohanim*, they read the first two *aliyot* and all the other *aliyot* are read by women. His reason is that "Where there is no alternative, [the consideration of] *kevod ha-tzibbur* is pushed aside"; i.e., if the *kohanim* were to read the portions normally reserved for non-*kohanim*, people might think that they were disqualified from the priesthood. Therefore, women should read in their place.[5] Such a ruling is inconceivable if the meaning of *kevod ha-tzibbur* is impure thoughts – better not to have the Torah read at all.

On the other hand, proof that *kevod ha-tzibbur* regarding women's readings has to do with an invidious contrast between literate women and seemingly illiterate men stems from the fact that the *rishonim* linked women's reading the Torah in the synagogue with *me'erah. Me'erah* (evil) is the imprecation invoked in the *beraita* in *Berachot* 20b and *Sukkah* 38a against someone who neglects to learn the text of *birkat ha-mazon* himself, and thus remains dependent on others:

---

who can read. In such a situation, the community's repute would suffer whether women read or not; better, then, to have women read than forgo the Torah reading altogether.

This explanation nicely parallels the usage of *kevod ha-tzibbur* in *Gittin* 60a: "One does not read the Torah in the synagogue from *chumashim* because of *kevod ha-tzibbur*," i.e., use of a scroll of a single book of the Torah such as *Bereishit, Shemot,* etc. is prohibited because here, too, a blot on the reputation of the community would result from the impression that the congregation was unable to afford, or uninterested in obtaining, a complete scroll containing all five books. On this and other aspects of *kevod ha-tzibbur, mechilah* of *kevod ha-tzibbur,* etc., see my Resp. *Bnei Banim*, vol. 2, nos. 10–11.

[4] *Sefer ha-Meorot* to *Berachot* 45a, and Rabbeinu Manoach in *Hilchot Berachot* 5:7.

[5] Resp. Maharam Rottenberg, Prague edition, no. 108; Mordechai to *Gittin, remez* 404; and Rabbeinu Yerucham 2:3. Maharam's ruling is not codified but his reasoning is not challenged; see *Bet Yosef, Orach Chayim* 135.

They clearly stated: a son recites [*birkat ha-mazon*] on behalf of his father, and a slave on behalf of his master, and a woman on behalf of her husband. But the Sages said: *Me'erah* be upon a man whose wife and children recite the blessing on his behalf.

R. Avraham Min ha-Har, in his commentary to *Megillah* 19b, writes concerning a woman reading the Purim *megillah* for men:

Certainly, *le-chatchilah* she should not fulfill men's responsibility [by reading the *megillah* for them], as is stated in [*Berachot*], "*Me'erah* be upon a man whose wife and children recite the blessing on his behalf." And it is stated in [*Megillah*]: "Everyone is counted towards the quorum of people who read the Torah, even a woman or a minor, but the Sages said, 'A woman may not read the Torah because of *kevod ha-tzibbur.*'"

Similarly, Ritva writes in *Megillah* 4a that although from a technical Halachic standpoint women can read the Purim *megillah* for men, "It is not *kevod ha-tzibbur*, and they are in the category of *me'erah*." R. Avraham Min ha-Har and the Ritva equate women's reading the *megillah* for men with women's reading the Torah for men (*kevod ha-tzibbur*), which they in turn compare to a man dependent on his wife or children to recite *birkat ha-mazon* for him (*me'erah*). The common denominator is that it is not *kevod* for men to be incompetent to read the texts themselves or to be perceived as incompetent. Impure thoughts (*hirhur*) are not mentioned at all.

A second unwarranted claim of sexual distraction as the grounds for a halacha can be found in an article by R. Aharon Feldman in a recent issue of *Tradition* magazine. He writes:

Even though there are opinions which permit women to recite *kaddish* in private prayer groups, these do not permit *kaddish* in the synagogue. The obvious reason for this, as explicitly stated by one rabbinic authority, is once again that men are easily distracted sexually by women, a fact which might affect their concentration on the prayers.[6]

Now, it should be obvious that from the standpoint of avoiding *hirhur* during prayers there is no difference between a private and public prayer group. In fact, the Mateh Efraim, who presumably is the authority referred to by R. Feldman, in his *Elef la-Mateh* prohibits a woman from raising her voice in *kaddish* or any other prayer whenever and wherever men are present:

> It is probable that she will try to prettify her voice (*le-visumi kala*), and we say: 'If women sing (*zamrei nashei*) and men respond, it is licentiousness'" (*Sotah* 48a).... It is worthy and proper that every respectable woman who fears G-d, whether married or single, not make her voice heard where there is [any] man. Only her lips should move [in prayer] but her voice should not be heard at all, lest the man who hears [her] be brought to *hirhur*... for she has to guard lest she be a stumbling-block for people.[7]

This would, perforce, equally apply to women's *aliyot*, to women's *zimmun*, and to women's reading the *megillah* – according to this *chumrah* all would be forbidden in the presence of men, lest the woman's voice cause sexual distraction. But such an approach is contradicted by the *rishonim*:

---

[6] *Tradition* 33/2 (winter 1999): 71. The article, "Halakhic Feminism or Feminist Halakha?" is an unremittingly negative review of the book *Jewish Legal Writings by Women*. Remarkably, however, R. Feldman passes over what to my mind is the book's most objectionable feature: the strident and at times insulting tone of a few of the articles. Particularly egregious is the article "Artificial Insemination of an Unmarried Woman," one of three written in Hebrew. It labels as racist objections to using non-Jewish sperm to father Jewish babies, and dismisses those who are concerned lest the availability of such insemination serve as a cover-up for promiscuity by irrelevantly citing the Talmudic dictum *"Kol ha-posel, be-mumo posel."*

[7] *Mateh Efraim* and *Elef la-Mateh, Dinei Kaddish Yatom* 4:8, and see below, notes 16–17. The language "It is worthy and proper..." is from *Eliyah Rabah* in the name of *Be'er Sheva*.

1. Maharam Rottenberg and the other *rishonim* who cite him, as well as *Sefer ha-Meorot*, R. Avraham Min ha-Har and Ritva, ignore *hirhur* in the case of women reading the Torah.

2. Ritva explicitly permits women to recite the *zimmun* and men to answer[8] and, according to Bach,[9] so does Ravad.

3. Rashi, Rambam, and many other *rishonim* permit women to read the Purim *megillah* for men unconditionally,[10] ignoring *hirhur*, and even *Halachot Gedolot* and most others who forbid it do so for reasons unconnected with *hirhur*.[11]

In the case of *kaddish*, Resp. *Chavot Yair*, the first authority to address the question of a woman saying *kaddish*, objected to it as undermining established customs,[12] but neither he nor any of the other *acharonim* of the

---

[8] Ritva, *Hilchot Berachot* 7:2.

[9] *Bayit Chadash* to 689. Both Ravad and Ritva view men and women as equally commanded in *birkat ha-mazon*, which is not the accepted Halachah, but this is irrelevant to their views on *hirhur*. On men answering to women's *zimmun*, see *Bnei Banim*, vol. 3, no. 1.

[10] Rashi on *Erchin* 3a; *Sefer ha-Meorot*; Riaz in *Shaltei ha-Giborim*, and Ritva, Meiri and *Nimukei Yosef*, all on *Megillah* 4a; *Or Zarua*, pt. 2, no. 368. These *rishonim* state explicitly that women may read for men. Others imply as much by quoting *Megillah* 4a or by mentioning, without qualification, women's obligation to read the *megillah*: see Rambam, *Hilchot Megillah* 1:1; Rif and Raban to *Megillah* 4a; *Shibolei ha-Leket* 198; *Ohel Moed, Dinei Megillah*, p. 108.

[11] *Halachot Gedolot*, Venice edition, p. 80; *Tosafot* in *Erchin* 3a; Ravyah chap. 569; Mordechai to *Megillah, remez* 778; *Sefer ha-Niyar*, Rosh, *Sefer ha-Agudah* and Ran (on the Rif), all to *Megillah* 4a; Rabbeinu Yerucham 10:2. Their reason is that women are not as fully obligated in the *megillah* reading as are men.

Only *Sefer ha-Kolbo*, chap. 45, and *Orchot Chayim* (both by the same author), prohibit women from reading the Purim *megillah* for men because of *kol be-ishah ervah*. This can be extended to *zimmun* because of the prevalence of drinking at meals, see *Sefer ha-Meorot* to *Megillah* 19b, but not to kaddish; and see *Bnei Banim*, vol. 2, no. 10 and, in English, my *Equality Lost: Essays in Torah Commentary, Halacha, and Jewish Thought* (Urim, 1999), chap. 7, and in note 14 there.

[12] Resp. *Chavot Yair*, no. 222.

seventeenth and eighteenth centuries who refer to it mentions sexual distraction. In our day, Resp. *Igrot Moshe* permits women occasionally to recite the *kaddish* in a men's *bet midrash* and writes that such has always been the custom.[13] He takes no account of *hirhur*.

The custom of saying *kaddish* in unison with other mourners is an additional factor. Elsewhere[14] I expanded on the ruling of my grandfather, R. Yosef Eliyahu Henkin *ztz"l*, permitting women to recite *kaddish* from the *ezrat nashim* together with male mourners, and buttressed his historical argument that in the time of the *Chavot Yair* at the end of the eighteenth century, Ashkenazi custom was for only one mourner to recite *kaddish* at a time. Under such circumstances, it was indeed objectionable for a woman to be the one person reciting *kaddish*. That was still the custom when *Mateh Efraim* was published in 1835, and that is what the author was referring to when he wrote "certainly it is forbidden, *chalilah*, for her to make her voice heard to the many (*le-hashmia kolah le-rabim*) in *kaddish*, whether in the synagogue or in a [private] *minyan*." Ashkenazi custom began to change to its current form of saying *kaddish* in unison only in the mid- to late nineteenth century.

It should be obvious that my grandfather, *Igrot Moshe*, and others are not saying that *hirhur* caused by a woman reciting *kaddish* is irrelevant. They are saying that a woman reciting *kaddish*, depending on the circumstances, does not cause *hirhur* at all, and that therefore other considerations can be addressed.[15] This is a *metziut* question, and it will not do for R. Feldman and

---

[13] Resp. *Igrot Mosheh, Orach Chayim*, V, no. 12 (2).

[14] *Bnei Banim*, vol. 2, no. 7 and vol. 3, no. 27, note; and my *Equality Lost*, chaps. 5–6.

[15] When a woman recites *kaddish* from behind the *mechitzah*, the only question of *tzniut* concerns her voice. If she is on the men's side a new set of questions arises, although here, too, *Igrot Moshe* seems unconcerned with *hirhur*. My grandfather wrote that although she should stand behind the *mechitzah*, if during *kaddish* she occasionally makes her way into the men's section, as long as there are males also saying *kaddish* "we ignore it" (*lo ichpat lan*); see *Teshuvot Ivra (Kitvei haGri"a Henkin*, vol. 2), no. 4 (2). It should be noted that the language used in no. 4 (1) *"bifnei ha-nashim"* does not indicate anything as to whether or not her voice is audible in the

others to simply cite *Mateh Efraim.* The question which has to be asked is this: Does a woman reciting the *kaddish* today really cause impure thoughts and sexual distraction among men? Where the answer is "yes" or "probably," one cannot rely on any *heter* in practice. In most communities, however, the answer is "no" or "very unlikely."

One reason that the recitation of the *kaddish* by women is not a source of sexual distraction in many of our communities – aside from fact that *kol be-ishah ervah* does not apply when *kaddish* is merely spoken[16] and doubtfully applies even when it is chanted[17] – is that we are inured to much worse. Inurement, or habituation, plays a significant if sometimes overlooked role in the development of Halacha. A trenchant example of this can be found in the *Yam shel Shlomoh* of R. Shlomo Luria, also known as Maharshal, to *Kiddushin* (4:25):

> Everything depends on what a person sees, and [if he] controls his impulses and can overcome them, he is permitted to speak to and look at an *ervah* (a woman forbidden to him) and inquire about her welfare. The whole world relies on this in using the services of and speaking to and looking at women.

Maharshal first relates to the individual, who may not go beyond what the Talmud permits in matters of *hirhur* unless he has extraordinary strengths

---

men's section. On the presence of a lone woman in the men's section see *Bnei Banim*, vol. 1, no. 4.

[16] See *Orach Chayim* 75:3 and *Magen Avraham* sub-par. 6. This is *Elef la-Mateh*'s meaning when he writes, "...even though *kol be-ishah ervah* does not apply...."

[17] *Elef la-Mateh* assumes that 1) chanting 2) the *kaddish*, a devotional text and 3) with men responding only *"amen"* and *"yehei shemei rabba,"* falls in the category of the provocative singing and response in *Sotah* 48; cf. *Bnei Banim* vol. 2, pp. 37–38 and vol. 3, no. 25 (2). [On *trei kali lo mishtam'ei* and other factors, see also *Bnei Banim* vol. 4, *maamar* 20.]

and qualities,[18] but concludes with the community: when the community (the "whole world") is accustomed to mingling with and speaking to women, their familiarity may be relied on to forestall sinful thoughts. The source for this distinction is the *Tosafot* in *Kiddushin* (82a). In the Gemara, *ha-kol le-shem shamayim* ("all in the name of heaven") is used by R. Acha bar Ada to explain the special liberty that he alone took in taking his betrothed granddaughter on his lap, but *Tosafot* comment, "On [*ha-kol le-shem shamayim*] we rely nowadays [in] that we make use of the services of [married] women." *Tosafot* employ this principle to justify widespread practices in their day. This is precisely the equation employed by Maharshal.

To prevent any mistake, it is important to be clear about which activities are subject to the mitigating effects of inurement and which are not. Habituation is an argument for permitting activities that are innocent in and of themselves, such as those mentioned by Maharshal: speaking to and casual sight of women[19] as well as everyday social and commercial activities that involve the mingling of the sexes. It is not an argument for permitting activities that have explicit or implicit sexual content, in which case *hirhur* is inevitable. Mixed swimming, especially by the scantily clad, is one example. Another is mixed dancing, particularly in discotheques. Two youngsters doing the Twist are not an acceptable couple even if they never touch.[20]

Besides *Tosafot*, another use by a *rishon* of the principle of habituation is apparently found in the fifteenth-century work *Leket Yosher*, in the name of his teacher, the author of *Terumat ha-Deshen*:

---

[18] This is the subject of a disagreement among *rishonim:* whether or not exceptionally pious individuals in every generation may take special liberties. See my *Equality Lost*, chap. 9.

[19] On the difference between seeing and gazing *(histaklut),* see *Shitah Mekubetzet* to *Ketubbot* 17a and *Yam shel Shlomoh* to *Ketubbot* 2:3 and *Kiddushin* 4:25. Maharshal's position appears to be that a brief glance at a woman was always permitted, and habituation would permit even lengthier seeing.

[20] Modern and even ballroom dancing should not be confused with the minuets and other stylized or processional forms of dancing popular in pre-modern Europe. On the dancing mentioned permissively in a few sources, see *Bnei Banim* vol. 1, no. 37 (4–10).

He said that it is permitted to walk behind of the wife of a
chaver or behind his mother because nowadays we are not all
that prohibited (*ein anu muzharin kol kach*) from walking
behind a woman.[21]

Walking behind a woman is forbidden by the Talmud in *Berachot* 61a.
What is the meaning of "nowadays we are not all that prohibited"? It means
that although the Talmud forbade men from walking behind women lest it
cause *hirhur*,[22] nowadays women go everywhere and we are used to walking
in back of them, so no *hirhur* results.[23]

Among other *acharonim* besides the Maharshal, the clearest use of the
principle that habituation obviates *hirhur* is found in the *Levush*, written by
the Maharshal's student, R. Mordechai Yafeh. It is customary to add the
phrase *she-ha-simchah bi-me'ono*, "in Whose abode is joy," in *zimmun* at the
festive meals following a wedding. However, the thirteenth-century *Sefer
Chassidim* specifically excludes feasts "where women sit among the men,
hirhur being present."[24] The Levush writes on this issue at the end of his
Minhagim:

We do not take care about [avoiding] mixed seating because
nowadays women are very common among men, and there
are relatively few sinful thoughts [about them] because they

---

21 *Leket Yosher, Yoreh Deah* 37.

22 R. Yehuda b. R. Binyamin (Rivevan) in *Berachot,* and Resp. Radbaz, II, no. 770.
Rashi gives a different reason, but it does not easily fit into the language of *Leket
Yosher.*

23 Resp. *Tzitz Eliezer,* IX, no. 50 (3). In section (2) he suggests an explanation for the
difference, implied in *Leket Yosher,* between walking behind the wife or mother of a
chaver and behind other women. I have suggested that the former can be relied upon
not to walk in a provocative manner; cf. the daughter of R. Chananiah b. Teradion
in *Avodah Zarah* 18a.

24 Par. 393.

seem to us like "white geese" due to the frequency of their being among us....[25]

This is identical to the approach found in the *Yam shel Shlomoh*, and indeed, *she-ha-simchah bi-me'ono* is today universally recited even in communities where there is mixed seating at *sheva berachot*.[26]

In recent times, the principle of habituation has been employed by the author of *Aruch ha-Shulchan*, R. Yechiel Michel Epstein.

One of the things that prohibits a man from reciting the *Shema* is viewing the uncovered hair of a married woman. Nevertheless, *Aruch ha-Shulchan* (*Orach Chayim* 75:7) writes:

> For many years Jewish women have been flagrant in this sin and go bareheaded.... Married women go about with [uncovered] hair like girls. Woe to us that this has occurred in our day! Nonetheless, by law it would appear that we are allowed to pray and say blessings facing their uncovered heads, since the majority go about this way and it has become like [normally] uncovered parts of her body, as the Mordechai wrote in the name of Ravyah: "All the things we have mentioned as being *ervah* [are] only in what is normally covered."

In other words, although it remains forbidden for married women to go bareheaded in public,[27] because they do so regardless of the prohibition,

---

[25] The reference is to *Berachot* 20a, where R. Gidel sat near the entrance to the mikveh as women exited. He justified himself by saying that to him they were like "white geese," i.e., he had no untoward thoughts.

[26] Maharshal himself, in *Yam shel Shelomoh* to *Ketubbot* (1:20), agrees with *Sefer Chassidim* on not saying *she-ha-simchah bi-me'ono* where there is mixed seating. The contradiction can be explained by the festive nature of a wedding feast which makes it more conducive to *hirhur* than other occasions. Alternatively, in *Ketubbot* Maharshal writes that "in my country... in most places" men and women feasted in separate rooms at *sheva berachot,* and therefore he had no cause to justify mixed seating there, as opposed to the custom recorded by *Levush*. See below, n. 29.

their hair is no longer an impediment to a man's reading the *Shema*. Since men are used to seeing it, women's hair no longer causes *hirhur*.

All this complicates the task of a *posek*. In several areas of *tzniut* and interaction between men and women there are not always fixed rules, and he may have to employ knowledge of the community, psychology, and sociology (which *poskim* always employed, long before the social sciences were given names) to determine what is permissible and what is not for a particular *tzibbur*. A writer for the *Jewish Observer*[28] found it impossible to accept that in the strictly Orthodox Germanic-Dutch (*Yekkishe*) communities before the Holocaust and in their remnants around the world afterwards, mixed seating at weddings and other social events,[29] mixed Torah *shiurim*, and even mixed handshakes were the norm.

---

[27] *Aruch ha-Shulchan* waives the impediment of a married woman's uncovered hair as regards a man's reading *Shema,* but forbids her going bareheaded: the two are distinct *halachot* stemming from separate Talmudic discussions in *Berachot* 24a and *Ketubbot* 72a. On the Halachic parameters of women's hair covering today, see *Bnei Banim*, vol. 3, nos. 21–24. On *Aruch ha-Shulchan*'s disagreement with *Mishnah Berurah* on the issue of uncovered hair, see *Bnei Banim*, vol. 3, no. 26 (6–7). On the authority of *Aruch ha-Shulchan* relative to that of *Mishnah Berurah*, see *Bnei Banim*, vol. 2, no. 8.

[28] Levi Reisman in the *Jewish Observer*, October 1998, p. 42. Reisman insisted that the Germanic communities' practices resulted from a "lapse in observance" without Halachic sanction, and that their rabbis disagreed but were powerless to object. *Bet Meir* in *Even ha-Ezer* 62 disproves the first assertion, and the second is countered by the fact that rabbis of known piety conducted mixed-seating weddings for their children, as in the case of the wedding of R. Eli Munk, the son of R. Azriel Munk of Berlin, to the daughter of the Hamburg Rav, a leading *posek* and champion of the strictest Orthodoxy. And while it is true that these practices are dying out as the result of the destruction of the home *kehillot* during the Holocaust, as recently as less than thirty years ago the rav of one of the major *Yekkishe* congregations in England arranged a mixed-seating wedding for his daughter. Reisman's assertions were part of a lengthy exchange between him and myself, part of which was printed by the *Jewish Observer*.

[29] On seating at weddings and other occasions, see *Bnei Banim*, vol. 1, no. 35, and *Otzar ha-Poskim* (vol. 17), sect. 62:13, pp. 106–107.

Certainly, what was acceptable there is not necessarily acceptable everywhere, and certainly, the principle of habituation has the potential of being abused and misused by the irresponsible. Applying it to *Halachot* that exist independently of *hirhur*, such as head-covering by married women or the requirement of a mechitzah[30] in the synagogue, is abuse and misuse, not to mention titillating literature or entertainment. But in that there is nothing new.

---

[30] The requirement of separate seating is derived in *Sukkah* 52a from Zechariah 12:12–14, which describes funerary orations where *hirhur* is presumed to be negligible. Another source is the design of the Temple which distinguished between the *Ezrat Yisrael* and *Ezrat Nashim*. See, at length, in B. Litwin's *Sanctity of the Synagogue*, and see my *Bnei Banim* vol. 1, nos. 1–3 and 35 (and my *RoCJWI*, chaps. 12–13); and for a different explanation, vol. 2, nos. 12–13.

CHAPTER THREE

ON THE (ALLEGED) HAZARDS OF HABITUATION

THE VIEW ASCRIBED to me[1] that "where men are habituated to women, *hirhur* concerns are no longer an issue…. One need not be concerned with erotic thoughts nowadays as much as in previous generations" is not mine. *Hirhur* is still an issue and the amount of sexual stimulation prevalent in today's society is greater than in previous ones. Consequently, however, the *threshold* needed to evoke *hirhur* is higher. For example, where women walk around in halter tops or less, a short-sleeved blouse is minimally provocative, and when pornography is rampant, viewing a woman's face is not titillating.

What of the concern that the proverbial "synagogue president in Peoria" might misconstrue such remarks as grounds to permit anything from mixed dancing to doing away with a *mechitzah* in the synagogue, and demand as much from his rabbi? I have every sympathy with honest concerns of this sort; however, the above concerns are wide off the mark. Specifically:

1. "Could not the thesis [concerning habituation] be applied to annul the laws of *yichud?*" No. *Yichud* (which is independent of *hirhur*) is a Torah prohibition according to most opinions, and not susceptible to modification. Even according to other

---

[1] By R. Emmanuel Feldman in *Tradition,* Fall 2000. (See also the Spring 2001 issue.)

opinions it is, at the least, a formal rabbinical enactment by an early *Sanhedrin* and would require a court of even greater stature to abrogate it.

2. So, too, concerning a *mechitzah* in the synagogue. According to one opinion,[2] the *mechitzah* in the synagogue is a Torah requirement, and while this can be disputed on the basis of Rashi's, Meiri's and *Maharsha*'s opinions that *mechitzah* is wholly a rabbinical enactment[3] – only the requirement for separate *seating* is prophetic in origin – the same restrictions on its abrogation would apply as above in 1. There is thus no chance of doing away with the *mechitzah* in the synagogue, *et al.*

Moreover, what I wrote refers to the accommodation of already prevalent practices and standards, not to the introduction of new ones. I made this point in *Equality Lost* (Urim, 1999, p. 82):

There is no Halachic imperative to introduce mingling of the sexes where it does not already exist. What we have said here... is not an agenda. It is much easier to legitimize existing practice than to justify new ones....

This continues the venerable Halachic practice of *limmud zechut* and *ex post facto* justification of community practices, which then become, via custom, functionally *le-chatchilah*. *Limmud zechut* usually involves the following elements: (1) an established or intractable practice (2) seemingly at variance with Halacha, which is (3) practiced by essentially Torah-observant communities and for which (4) grounds or support can indeed be found, even if initially we might prefer otherwise.

Determining when these conditions are met is the responsibility of the *poskim* on the scene. They can be met in the case of increased mingling of

---

[2] Resp. *Igrot Moshe, Orach Chayim,* part 1 no. 39.

[3] See *Bnei Banim,* vol. 1, no. 3 [translated in *Responsa on Contemporary Jewish Women's Issues,* chaps. 12–13].

the sexes, as I illustrated with the case of the Germanic-Dutch *Yekkishe* communities. They are not met in the case of abolishing the *mechitzah,* since for some two hundred years, maintaining a *mechitzah* has been a litmus test of membership in the Orthodox community. Communities that adopted mixed pews invariably went on to dispense with Halachic Judaism altogether.

Lastly, R. Feldman raised an all-purpose objection based on *lo plug,* the principle that exceptions are not made in applying rabbinical enactments. But if *lo plug* applied here, R. Acha could not have lifted a bride on his shoulders and R. Gidel and R. Yochanan would not have sat at the entrance to a women's mikveh! Likewise, *Semak,* Meiri and Ritva could not have permitted exceptional individuals even in post-Talmudic times to exempt themselves from many of the strictures regarding *hirhur.*

In fact, determining when *lo plug* does apply is a complicated matter; see the controversies among the *acharonim* in *Orach Chayim* 275 regarding not reading by lamplight on Shabbat, lest one inadvertently regulate the flame. Specifically concerning *hirhur,* Resp. *Radbaz,* part 2 no. 770, wrote regarding the prohibition of walking behind a woman that all women in all countries are the same, but he did not write that all men are the same. This distinction between who is subject to an enactment (men) and what or whom the enactment is about (women), with only the latter being subject to *lo plug,* is also made by the *Taz* and cited by *Biur Halachah* in 275.

In the second half of his critique R. Feldman assesses my sources, starting with the Maharshal who, he states, permits only what was permitted in the first place and who does not mention habituation. He notes that Maharshal quotes from the Ritva that the leniency of *ha-kol le-shem shamayim* should be used only by a great *hasid* (saint), and concludes that "this leniency can hardly be widely applied nowadays." In a footnote, he writes that when Maharshal says that the "whole world" relies on this leniency, "he is merely stating that the practice is widespread and nothing more." If R. Feldman fails to notice the contradiction in his argument – a leniency which "can hardly be widely applied" cannot at the same time be described as "widespread" – then clearly I need to restate my central point in greater detail.

In *Kiddushin* 91b, R. Acha b. Aba took the unusual step of taking his already-betrothed, prepubescent granddaughter in his lap (some say under his bedclothes). When challenged by his son-in-law, he justified himself by citing a statement of Shmuel, *"Ha-kol le-shem shamayim"* (everything [done] for the sake of Heaven [is permissible]), i.e., he had no untoward thoughts. This fits in with other seemingly egregious behavior by sages who justified themselves similarly, such as R. Acha in *Ketuvot* 17a who danced at a wedding with the bride on his shoulders, and R. Gidel in *Berachot* 20a who sat near the entrance to the mikveh while the women exited, each explaining that women were to him like a "wooden beam" or like "white geese" rather than sexual objects. Similarly, in *Shabbat* 13a, Ulla was in the habit of kissing his married sisters on their hands or sleeves or perhaps on their bodices, a practice he forbade to others. Tosafot there explains that Ulla was a completely righteous person (*tzaddik gamur*), and "he knew that he himself would not come to *hirhur*" even though others might.

That *ha-kol le-shem shamayim* is identical to statements that women are like wooden beams or white geese is explicit in *Tosfot Rabbeinu Elchanan* (the son of Ri *Ba'al ha-Tosafot*) in *Avodah Zarah* 17a, regarding Ulla:

> He permitted himself [to kiss his sister(s)] because she was like a wooden beam to him, as we say in *Ketuvot* about [dancing with] a bride and as we say at the end of *Kiddushin* "I hold like Shmuel's statement [that] *ha-kol le-shem shamayim.*"

How, then, are we to understand the comment by Tosafot in *Kiddushin* 92a on *ha-kol le-shem shamayim*: "On this we rely today in using the services of women"? Why not say that since R. Acha b. Aba was a *tzaddik gamur* like R. Acha, R. Gidel, and Ulla, he was permitted what remained forbidden to everyone else? Similarly, *Maharshal's* heading in *Yam shel Shelomoh* there, following Tosafot, is "the whole world relies on this [*ha-kol le-shem shamayim*] in using the service of, speaking to, and looking at women." The "we" in Tosafot is "the whole world" in Maharshal, i.e., the general community. Yet the ability of a *tzaddik gamur* to refrain from *hirhur* says nothing about the average person. Maharshal himself, after citing Tosafot, cites the Ritva that one should not permit himself leniencies in matters of *hirhur* unless he is a saint.

Accordingly, R. Feldman gets things backwards when he writes,

> The [Talmudic] passage states that contact with women is permitted where it is done *ha-kol le-shem shamayim* (the intention is for godly [noble] purposes). This passage refers to contact with totally platonic intentions.... According to the text, platonic relations are permitted because they were never forbidden in the first place.

Rather, the question is not whether platonic relations are permitted, but who is entitled to claim that his contacts with women are platonic, and in what circumstances.

On this basis I explained Tosafot's reasoning as being that the "we" of "on this we rely today" are equivalent in status to R. Acha b. Aba with regard to *ha-kol le-shem shamayim*, i. e., when the community at large is accustomed to mingling with and speaking to women, their familiarity can be relied upon to forestall sinful thoughts. I cited the *Levush* and Resp. *Tzitz Eliezer*'s explanation of the *Leket Yosher* (Resp. *Tzitz Eliezer* also cites the *Levush*) as evidence that such a rationale is, indeed, found in Halachic literature. All the citations reinforce each other: the Tosafot is the source for the *Yam shel Shelomoh,* while the latter helps in understanding the Tosafot; the *Levush* helps explain the Tosafot, while the Tosafot provides sanction for the *Levush*; and so, too, the words of *Yam shel Shelomoh* and the *Levush,* Maharshal's disciple, illuminate and reinforce each other. Finally, the example of the Germanic-Dutch Orthodox communities provides a concrete illustration of the principle of the Tosafot and Maharshal put into actual practice.

R. Feldman barely cites the Gemara, omits mention of Tosafot altogether, and makes only passing reference to the practices of the Germanic-Dutch communities ("the practice of some pre-war German rabbis to shake hands with women" – as if that were all there was to it). The

Tosafot in *halachah* and the Germanic-Dutch communities in *ma'aseh* are the two pillars of my "thesis," as R. Feldman calls it, but he ignores them and instead snipes at my subsidiary sources.

Two additional points, however, deserve independent consideration. The first is: what is the meaning of the *Levush*'s statement[4] that when women frequently intermingle with men, "there are relatively few sinful thoughts" (*ein kan hirhurei averah kol kach*)? Is not even a small amount of erotic thought forbidden? But see *Levush* in *Even ha-Ezer* 64:2:

> It is permitted to look at the jewelry on [the bride] and at her uncovered hair, for this does not cause *hirhur* so much (*eino mevi col kach li-yedei hirhur*); therefore, it is permitted [to do so] in order to praise and value her, even though with other women this, too, is prohibited.

It means that most of the time, gazing at the bride's hair and jewels does not result in *hirhur,* and therefore it is permitted when done for a good reason. So, too, when men and women habitually intermingle, most of the time no *hirhur* stems from the intermingling itself. But what about the minority of times? I suggest that the *Levush* is referring to a fact of life. To attempt to prevent *hirhur* completely is futile; *hirhur averah* is one of the things no one escapes daily, as stated in *Bava Batra* 164b. Men will occasionally come to *hirhur* no matter what, and certainly adolescents, whom Rashi in *Sukkah* 26a describes as "prone to *hirhur*" (*she-ha-hirhur matzuy bahem*).

Hirhur can result from gazing even at a woman's little finger, as in *Berachot* 24a. Even if she is completely clothed from head to foot, *hirhur* can still result from seeing her walking, as in Resp. *Radbaz* above; to forestall it, she would have to walk inside a barrel or, better yet, to never appear in public at all. Midrash *Tanchuma* in *Vayishlach*, in fact, reaches that conclusion, "...a woman should stay inside her home and not go out in the street... lest she be a stumbling-block to men who, as a result, will look at a woman." But that is not Halachah, and no community practices it.

---

[4] In *Minhagim* at the end of *Orach Chayim*.

The second question is more difficult: if habituation helps to forestall *hirhur*, why did the *Levush* comment on it only regarding *she-ha-simcha bi-me'ono*,[5] and not in *Even ha-Ezer* 21:1–3 regarding the prohibitions of walking behind, listening to the voice of, and seeing the hair of a woman?

Note a further question, however: the *Levush* mentions the issue only in his supplementary *Minhagim* ("Customs"); why not in its proper place in *Even ha-Ezer* 62, where the laws of saying *she-ha-simcha bi-me'ono* are found? Another puzzle: why did *Aruch ha-Shulchan* in *Even ha-Ezer* (and anywhere else) omit mention both of the stringency of *Sefer Chassidim* and the leniency of the *Levush* – *mimah nafshecha*? It is not his way to overlook a *halachah* so featured in the *acharonim*.

Certainly, there are limits to argument-from-omission, whether omitted by the *Levush* or by the *Aruch ha-Shulchan*, and speculation as to the reasons remains exactly that. But *Levush* and *Aruch ha-Shulchan* both wrote comprehensive works they hoped would largely supersede the *Shulchan Aruch* (!), as they stated in their respective introductions; *Aruch ha-Shulchan* even wrote that he was following in the path of the *Levush* in this regard. They included everything discussed by the *poskim* up until their times, including established customs. Perhaps they did not include in the body of their codes (as opposed to in the *Minhagim* of the *Levush*) either the non-Talmudic stringency of *Sefer Chassidim* regarding *she-ha-simcha bi-me'ono* or the countervailing local custom, because the one and the other were not fixed but varied from place to place and from generation to generation. So too, there was no question of codifying exceptions to the Talmudic laws of *Even ha-Ezer* 21, which, however, does not preclude the existence of such exceptions.

---

[5] See above, chap. 2.

PART II

CHAPTER FOUR

IS A HANDSHAKE A TORAH VIOLATION?

TOUCHING

As OPPOSED TO ANY touching at all between husband and wife when she is in a state of *niddah*, which is explicitly forbidden in the *Shulchan Aruch*,[1] no such sweeping prohibition of all physical contact is found in relation to other *'arayot*. Thus, while the *Shulchan Aruch* [2] forbids numerous forms of interaction with *'arayot* including winks and gestures and pleasurable gazing, simple touching without intention of affect is not one of them. As our generation's *Sheurei Shevet ha-Levi* on *Hilchot Niddah*[3] writes:

> [He may] not touch her [i.e., his *niddah* wife]: that is to say, even without intention of desire and affection, while [in their absence] even a rabbinical prohibition does not apply in [touching other] *'arayot*.

---

[1] *Yoreh Deah* 195:2: "[He may] not touch her even [with his] little finger" (or, "…even [on her] little finger").

[2] *Even ha-Ezer* 21:1.

[3] By R. Shmuel Vozner, 3rd edition (5758), p. 252.

So, too, the *Taz*[4] mentions: "...his friend's wife [with whom] he is forbidden to sleep in one bed, but [non-affectionate] touching is permitted."

A graphic example of rabbinic permission for even extended touching between men and a married woman, in circumstances not reflecting "desire and affection," can be found, according to a number of *rishonim*, in *Beitzah* 25b. There R. Nachman permitted his wife Yalta to "go out on an *alonki*." Rashi explained that a man placed his hand on his partner's shoulder and his partner placed his own hand on the first's shoulder, thus forming a place to sit for a third person who sat "on his chair on their arms," and according to this it is at least possible that Yalta sat on a chair carried by men, without direct physical contact between them.[5]

Meiri,[6] however, explained that she sat directly on their arms without a chair, and such is the implication of R. Chananel who explained *alonki* as being a "shoulder saddle" without mention of a chair. Moreover, the *Aruch*,[7] after quoting R. Chananel, added that "a woman is afraid lest she fall, [and] for that reason she was permitted to shoulder *(lekatef)* by supporting herself with her hands on their heads, and [so] she did not fall."[8]

All this, of course, does not constitute permission for members of opposite sexes to casually touch each other. Particularly in our society and particularly among the young, the tendency, if not the inevitability, of one thing leading to another is too great to allow for any breach of a rigid policy

---

[4] *Orach Chayim* 615:1. The *Taz* takes for granted that about which Resp. *Pnei Yehoshua*, pt. 2 no. 44, wrote "it is possible" *(efshar)*.

[5] This may be the source of the custom at weddings to lift the chair on which the bride is seated, even by men. It might also explain R. Acha's carrying a bride on his shoulders in *Ketubbot* 17a. Even if R. Acha was a saint for whom the bride was like a "wooden beam," what gave him the idea to do such a thing in the first place? If, however, it was accepted practice to lift the bride on a chair, he simply took things a step further and carried her without a chair.

[6] *Beitzah, loc. cit.* It should be noted that Meiri, in *Avodah Zarah* 17a, follows the opinion of Rambam concerning *lo tikrevu* (discussed below).

[7] *S.v. alonki.*

[8] For further discussion of this *sugya*, see my *Bnei Banim*, vol. 4, no. 11, p. 39.

of *shomer negiah*, under the rubric of *Sechor, sechor, amrinan le-nezira – le-karmecha lo tikrav.*[9]

LO TIKREVU

Rambam famously applied a Torah prohibition not only to sexual relations but also to pre- and proto-sexual behavior such as kissing and hugging. While actual relations with an *ervah* are prohibited under penalty of *karet*, kissing and other similar acts are an infraction of a negative commandment, punishable by flogging. This is based on the language of *Vayikra* 18:6 concerning *'arayot* in general, and of 18:19 concerning a *niddah*: instead of simply prohibiting relations with them, the Torah warns "*lo tikrevu*" (plural) in the first verse and "*lo tikrav*" (singular) in the second, meaning "you shall not come close" i.e., foreplay. I use the term "foreplay" in its broadest sense – action or even speech of a sexual nature, of the sort that serves as a preliminary to or accompaniment of sexual relations.

This proviso precludes social handshakes from being subsumed under the *lo ta'aseh*, since a handshake is not a preliminary to relations. This is so even if the handshake includes an element of affection or pleasure; affection alone without the feature of desire is not a Torah violation. The *Shach*[10] already wrote this when he stipulated "the way of desire and affection of intercourse" (*derech taavah ve-chibat biah*) rather than simply "affection."

There is clear proof of this distinction in *Sefer ha-Mitzvot* of the Rambam[11] in R. Chaim Heller's translation, also found word-for-word in the *Sefer Mitzvah* of *Sefer ha-Batim*[12]:

---

[9] A Talmudic idiom for not leading oneself into temptation, literally: "'Go around, go around,' we say to the Nazirite [who is forbidden to drink wine]. 'Don't approach your vineyard!'"

[10] *Yoreh Deah*, 195:20, and in greater detail in 157:10:

"משמע דאף הרמב"ם לא קאמר אלא כשעושה חיבוק ונישוק דרך חיבת ביאה... וכן כתב הסמ"ג והכתר תורה שם אלמא דלא לוקה אלא בדרך תאווה וחיבת ביאה, וזהו דלא כבית יוסף...."

See languages of Rambam, below; see also Resp. *Lev Chayim* (Palaggi), pt. 2 no 4, "נגיעה בעלמא לא שמענו".

[11] *Lo Ta'aseh* 353.

We are warned not to come close to any of these *'arayot* even without intercourse, such as hugging and kissing and which resembles them from among the promiscuous activities *(mipe'ulot ha-zenut)*.[13]

Rambam himself used similar language in his *Mishneh Torah, Hilchot Sanhedrin* 19:4[14]: "One who comes close *(ha-karev)* to *'arayot* in any of the ways of promiscuity *(mi-darchei ha-zenut)*...." Certainly, handshaking is not counted among *pe'ulot* or *darchei ha-zenut*. Moreover, in both *Sefer ha-Mitzvot*[15] and *Hilchot Issurei Biah*[16] 21:1 Rambam stresses that the *lo ta'aseh* prohibits activities that customarily accompany sexual relations.[17] Handshaking is not one of these.

Further evidence comes from the *Terumat ha-Deshen*,[18] who distinguishes between "other distancings *(perishot)*, that he not touch her" and "huggings

---

[12] By R. David Kochavi, written in the fourteenth century. His works are based on those of Rambam.

[13] Or, "*mi-ma'asei ha-hit'alsut* (from the acts of lovemaking)" – R. Yosef Kapach, *Sefer Kedushah*, p. 21, note 41.

[14] No. 162; Rambam there lists *lo tikrevu* as one of the 207 Torah prohibitions incurring *malkot*.

[15] ‏"לשון ספרא, כאילו יאמר לא תקרבו שום קירוב שיביא לגלות ערוה"‏

[16] ‏"כל הבא על ערוה מן העריות דרך אברים או שחיבק ונישק דרך תאוה ונהנה מקירוב בשר" הרי זה לוקה מן התורה, שנאמר... לא תקרבו לגלות ערוה, כלומר לא תקרבו לדברים המביאים לידי גילוי ערוה"‏

Resp. *Igrot Moshe, EH* 1:56 and 2:14 (dated eight days apart) defines the *lav*, too, as ‏קריבה והכנה למעשה זנות, דבר המביא לידי גלוי ערוה‏ etc. However, he is equivocal regarding handshakes; see 1:56 (end)

‏ומה שראית שיש מקילין אף מיראי ה' ליתן יד לאשה כשהיא מושיטה, אולי סוברין דאין זו דרך חבה ותאוה אבל למעשה קשה לסמוך על זה.‏

And see below, n. 22.

[17] Cf. especially *Megillat Esther* on *Sefer ha-Mitzvot*: "The Torah only forbade *keruv shel gilui arayot*, that is, what [people] normally do when they wish to have relations...."

[18] *Terumat ha-Deshen, Teshuvot* no. 250. See also *Sefer Raban*, no. 334.

and kissings,[19] which [people] have pleasure from as from relations (*de-nehenim meihem kemo mi-tashmish*)." A handshake is certainly not in the category of *kemo mi-tashmish*.[20]

Finally, Rambam in *Hilchot Issurei Biah* 11:9 writes, regarding one's *niddah* wife, that one may "not touch her because of occasion for sin (*hergel davar*)," i.e., touching is prohibited rabbinically because of what it can lead to, but the touching is not itself a Torah violation. This in spite of the fact that Rambam in 21:4 classifies a *niddah* as *ervah*.

THE CONTROVERSY

In the wider religious community, nevertheless, handshaking between men and women remains controversial. Some rabbis will shake a woman's hand when it is extended to them, while others demur even at the cost of embarrassing the woman. The reason for the latter practice is often given[21] as follows:

Bet Yosef[22] cites a *teshuva* of the Rashba[23] concerning taking the pulse of one's wife during her menses, which begins "it is possible that all coming

---

[19] See *Eitz Chayim, Hilchot Niddah u-She'ar 'Arayot*, ch. 12 שחבק ונשק דרך תאוה בקירוב בשר; also see Radbaz in *Metzudat David, Mitzvah* 160, who wrote "hugging, kissing and embracing (*gifuf*)."

[20] Neither, apparently, is handholding in dancing. See *Bnei Banim,* vol. 1 no. 37 (8–9) that among early *acharonim* – Resp. *Mahardach, Binyamin Ze'ev* and others who forbade mixed dancing, none explained that dancing while holding hands can itself constitute a violation of *lo tikrevu*. Compare the pamphlet *Geder Olam* from 5650 by a rabbi in Warsaw (later mislabeled as being by the *Chafetz Chayim*) who wrote in conclusion (p. 39): "It is common that one also violates, as a result of the dance, the *lav* of *lo tikrevu;* sometimes they kiss and hug one another during the dance because the evil inclination burns within him and violates this *lav*"; ergo, without the added factor of kissing and hugging the *lav* is not violated. (Contrast Resp. *Igrot Moshe, EH* 2:13 – unless the reference is to ballroom dancing, which involves embracing.)

[21] See *Bet Shmuel, Even ha-Ezer* 20:1; *Torat ha-Shlamim Yoreh Deah* 195:15; *Sdei Chemed* section *Chatan, kallah ve-chupah*, chapter 12.

[22] *Yoreh Deah* 195.

[23] *Teshuvot ha-Rashba ha-Meyuchasot la-Ramban,* no. 127, originally attributed to Ramban (Nachmanides). The *teshuvah* itself does not mention Rambam

close (*krevah*) is forbidden by the Torah." Presumably, this refers to the Rambam's opinion. Yet taking the pulse of one's wife certainly does not indicate *chibat biah*! According to this understanding, Rambam prohibits all physical contact with an *ervah* by Torah law.

How this accords with the wording of the Rambam himself – specifically cited by *Shach* as his reason for disagreeing with the *Bet Yosef* – remains unexplained.

However, in *Bnei Banim*[24] I demonstrated that the Rashba was probably referring not to Rambam but rather to Rabbeinu Yonah, Rashba's primary teacher. R. Yonah is the one *rishon* who wrote explicitly that any touching at all of an *ervah* violates *lo tikrevu* and is *yehareg ve-al ya'avor*.[25] But there are no grounds to interpret Rambam in the same fashion. In my opinion, those who wish to follow R. Yonah's[26] stringent ruling may do so, but without claiming that this is basic Halachah.

(Maimonides), but *Bet Yosef* assumed that it was stating Rambam's position. *Bet Shmuel* even wrote that the *teshuvah* mentions Rambam by name ("*ve-katav ba-teshuvah*"), and thus needlessly rejected the *Shach*, who had rejected *Bet Yosef* on account of Rambam's own language in *Sefer ha-Mitzvot* and *Hilchot Issurei Biah*. Following the *Bet Shmuel*, *Torat ha-Shlamim*, *Sdei Chemed* and others all wrote that the *teshuvah* mentions Rambam (which it does not).

Presumably, the *Chazon Ish* followed their lead. Resp. *Igrot Moshe* in *EH* 2:14 initially wrote that the *teshuvah* mentions Rambam, but in *YD* 3:54:2, written nine years later, he noted that the Ramban (i.e., the Rashba) doesn't mention Rambam; see *ad loc.*, and see below.

24 Vol. 1, *loc. cit.*

25 *Igeret ha-Teshuvah, Yom Bet*, quoted in *Orchot Chayim* pt. 2, *Hilchot Biot Assurot* (p. 112). Rashba himself does not agree; see Resp. Rashba, vol. 1, no. 1,188.

26 There are *two* versions of R. Yonah's view. In *Shaarei Teshuvah*, pt. 3, par. 80, he forbade "all flesh contact, such as touching the hand of a married woman." In *Igeret ha-Teshuvah*, however, he added a condition "in order to receive pleasure (*keday lehanot*) from the touch," i.e., touching is a violation of *lo tikrevu* only if done with the intention of enjoyment, but not when returning a handshake out of politeness or in order to avoid embarrassing the woman.

CHAPTER FIVE

RESPONSE TO "WOMEN'S *ALIYOT* IN CONTEMPORARY SYNAGOGUES"

THREE POSITIONS are presented in Rabbi Gideon Rothstein's article "Women's *Aliyot* in Contemporary Synagogues," submitted to *Tradition* magazine:

1. Rabbi Mendel Shapiro's stance that women's aliyot should be permitted anytime and anywhere a congregation so wishes.

2. Rabbi Rothstein's reaction, that women's *aliyot* should never be permitted.

3. My opinion that a *heter* can be established, but that in practice women's *aliyot* are outside the consensus and, I predict, will remain so for the foreseeable future. There will be those who confuse prediction with predilection; nevertheless, I will limit my comments on Rabbi Rothstein's essay to what directly pertains to me.

First, the author has his chronology wrong. He writes:

> R. Henkin's reasoning supports [R.] Shapiro's claim that the
> institution of *ba'al keriah* should take away the problem [of
> *kevod ha-tzibbur*]. Since the men are being read for [and don't
> read themselves], a woman's standing next to the *ba'al keriah*
> should mean nothing more than [if] a man [was doing so].

I did not second Rabbi Shapiro's argument, for in the first place he got it
from *Bnei Banim*, vol. 2 no. 10. Rabbi Rothstein subsequently comments that
I "accepted *or anticipated*" Shapiro's "basic reasoning." And while confusion
on this point could result from reading only the exchange between Rabbi
Shapiro and myself in the *Edah Journal* (vol. 1 no. 2), Rabbi Rothstein should
know better, since he himself cites *Bnei Banim*.

The author writes further: "R. Henkin explicitly rejects the difference
between temporary and permanent surrender of 'dignity' (*kevod ha-tzibbur*),
without supporting proof or argumentation...." This ascribes to me a failure
to distinguish between *sha'at de-chak* and normal circumstances, which would
be remarkable were it true.

Where did Rabbi Rothstein get the idea that I held such an opinion? He
cites *Bnei Banim*, volume 2:11, but without a page number. Perhaps the
explanation is as follows: He saw what I wrote in page 51 regarding *kevod
tzibbur*: "Where have we found that it is permissible to read *be-akrai* from
chumashim, or for a woman to read *be-akrai* from the Torah?" But he
misinterpreted *be-akrai* to mean "temporarily" (*arai*) rather than "randomly"
or "by chance occurrence," and that accounts for his comment. It should
also be noted that my rhetorical question, "Where have we found..." (*heichan
matzinu*) is an accepted form of argumentation, contrary to his charge that I
brought none.

The author further disagrees with my speculation on the need for
unanimous waiver of *kevod tzibbur* by the congregation, but overlooks the
fact that I suggested it not as my own view, but in order to explain *Sefer ha-
Batim*'s singular opinion that distinguishes between a synagogue venue and
that of a private home and permits women's *aliyot* in the latter. Concerning
unanimity, R. Rothstein writes:

Aside from failing to provide any supporting evidence for that position, [R.] Henkin also fails to support his further claim that only occasional and private services have implicit unanimous consent.

But I did not "fail" in an attempt to support a claim, but rather stressed the need for further corroboration. Moreover, I cited analogous cases. One is the *Mishnah* in *Peah* (4:1): "Even if ninety-nine [poor people] want [the field's owner] to distribute [the grain from the corner of the field reserved for the poor] and only one of them wants to grab [it directly], we listen to him because he opted for the Halachah," i.e., unanimous consent is needed for change.

A more exact parallel can be found in *Shulchan Aruch Orach Chayim* (153:6–7) which distinguishes between a *shtiebel* or a synagogue in a village and a synagogue in a large town. Congregants may sell the former house of worship but not the latter, the reason being that the town's synagogue is considered as having been built in trust for the many visitors from all over who will pray in it, and as *Mishnah Berurah* explains, "perhaps there is even one [former worshipper] from the end of the world who does not agree to the sale." Consent by all past and present worshippers cannot be assumed, and without such unanimity the sale cannot go through. However, if the synagogue was built subject to the dictates of an individual — *kal va-chomer* if it is located in his own home — he may do as he likes.

The similarity between this and *Sefer ha-Batim*'s allowing women's *aliyot* in a private home but not in a regular synagogue is clear. What is not clear is why R. Rothstein claims that I produced no support for the concept of unanimous *mechila*.[1]

---

[1] Which cannot be assumed in the average community. Picture a community with a central synagogue as well as a private service in a home. Most people attend the synagogue services and would need a reason *not* to. By contrast, attendance at the private service involves a conscious decision, and if *aliyot* are granted there to women, attendance implies consent. This would not apply should the synagogue itself institute women's *aliyot*: in that case, all that those who continue to worship

Finally, in my response to Rabbi Shapiro in the *Edah Journal* and later in *Bnei Banim*, volume four, I had proposed that *kevod tzibbur* would not be a factor on *Simchat Torah*: since according to our *minhag* every male receives an *aliyah*, women's *aliyot* at that time cannot be construed as indicating that some men are incapable of doing so.[2]

Rabbi Rothstein objects to this:

> [R.] Henkin is too quick to assume that only *Simhat Torah* does not imply ignorance. Consider, for example, a case

---

there proves is that there is a lack of an alternative synagogue in town, and consent to women's *aliyot* cannot be inferred.

[2] I explained in *Bnei Banim* 4:2, page 16, that according to the *baraita* in *Megilla* 23a women are not included in the count of seven *olim* to the Torah because of *kevod tzibbur*, but the text is silent regarding additional *aliyot*. Following the rationale of the *rishonim* that *kevod tzibbur* entails avoiding the appearance that not enough men know how to read from the Torah and that therefore they called up a woman, it would seem that this would apply only to the mandatory seven readers, but not to additional *aliyot* which are optional.

However, it can be objected that for a woman to read part of the obligatory reading, and thereby help discharge the congregation's obligation, is prohibited because of *kevod tzibbur* even if the reading is divided into more than seven parts. This hinges on the disagreement between the *Shulchan Aruch* and Rema in *Orach Chayim* 282:2. According to the former, it is permitted to add to the number of readers and read over with a blessing what was already read, and this is the Sephardic custom. In this way there might be no concern about *kevod tzibbur*, if in addition to the seven readers a woman would read in repetition of what was already read, since the *tzibbur* doesn't need her reading at all.

On *Simchat Torah*, however, it appears that one can be lenient even according to the Rema – who at other times prohibits repetitive readings with a blessing – since even Ashkenazic custom is to read from the beginning of *Ve-Zot ha-Brachah* until *me'onah elokei kedem* numerous times – and all the more so according to the custom that every male in the synagogue is called up to the Torah – since in that case it is impossible to think that there are men who don't know how, since they all do. In addition, the circumstances surrounding reading the Torah are already so different on *Simchat Torah* that it is unlikely that enabling women's *aliyot* then would lead to women's *aliyot* the rest of the year.

where it is absolutely obvious that the assembled men know how to read on their own – a convention of professional Torah readers, for example.

But following the definition I adduced from R. Avraham Min ha-Har and the Ritva, and which is the only definition clearly found in the *rishonim*, *kevod tzibbur* is a matter of how visitors and *outsiders* might misjudge the Torah literacy of the men of the community were women to receive *aliyot*. It is not a matter of how the residents view themselves; they in any case know who among them are able or unable to *lein*. This is also independent of whether or not visitors and outsiders are actually present at any particular reading of the Torah. Otherwise, any synagogue where all the men were in fact Torah-literate and no visitors were present could call up women at will, which no one has ever suggested.

At a "convention of professional Torah readers," in addition, in what way is it "absolutely obvious" whom and what they are? Nothing the outsider sees identifies them as being all *ba'alei kri'ah* other than, perhaps, convention hats or nametags, which are hardly sufficient to vitiate a rabbinical decree.

There are also a number of tangential comments to be made, and I will give only an example. R. Rothstein writes concerning the *me'era* curse on one who relies on his wife or children to read *birkat ha-mazon* to him:

> [R.] Henkin's reading of Ritva, though, sees the Sages as responding to the wrong problem. If the Sages were bothered by the man's ignorance, they should have turned their harsh language against the ignorance itself ("cursed be the man who does not know how to recite Grace"), not on his relying on others for assistance.

But I think there is no cause to curse a man just because he is ignorant, as he may never have had anyone to learn from. The curse applies specifically to one whose *wife and children* read for him, because he has close family members available to learn from, and his not having done so therefore indicates negligence or lack of interest.

CHAPTER SIX

BLIND SPOTS AND WOMEN'S ISSUES

SOMETIMES WE FIND ideological blind spots that make it difficult for people to deal with certain issues objectively. Two recent instances come to mind. In the first, two rabbis reportedly forbade women to dance with a *Sefer Torah* because of a "sub-prohibition of *be-chukoteihem*,[1]" as a result of its feminist origins.

Now, one can be against such dancing for other reasons,[2] but in order to invoke *be-chukoteihem* certain conditions apply. *Be-chukoteihem* pertains only to actions, as is written: "*Ke-ma'aseh eretz mitzrayim… u-ve-chukoteihem lo telechu*" (*Vayikra* 18:3). When there is no *ma'aseh* (action) there is no *be-chukoteihem*, as R. Yaakov Emden[3] wrote concerning monogamy. This applies even when the result resembles the situation among the nations, as in not taking a second wife (R. Emden's example), or allowing one's hair to grow long and unkempt[4]: since only a *shev ve-al ta'aseh* is involved – not marrying a second wife, not cutting or combing one's hair – *be-chukoteihem* is not involved.

---

[1] "*U-ve-chukotehem lo telechu* (you shall not follow their [the nations'] ordinances)" – the Torah prohibition against mimicking non-Jewish practices.

[2] But not on account of their being *niddot,* see *Yoreh Deah* 282:9.

[3] *She'elot Ya'avetz,* pt. 2 no. 15.

[4] See *Bnei Banim,* vol. 1 no. 7.

Removing one's *kipah* in public is an action and thus violates *be-chukoteihem* (according to the *Taz*[5]) but simply not putting it on does not. All this applies even when the results of our non-activity resemble what is found among the nations.

This is doubly the case when there is no *ke-ma'aseh eretz mitzrayim* to mimic at all. In the case of women dancing with a *Sefer Torah* there is no parallel phenomenon in non-Jewish society, and therefore no *be-chukoteihem*. This is so even according to the Gra.[6] According to the Maharik and the Rema, even without this reason *be-chukoteihem* does not apply because there is a rational reason (*ta'am*) involved, of wanting to express affection for the Torah. The idea of a "sub-prohibition" of *be-chukoteihem* applying to feminist motivations independent of actions is an invention.

A second example pertains to women rendering Halachic decisions. *Sefer ha-Chinuch,*[7] *Birkei Yosef* [8] and *Minchat Chinuch*[9] all allow it, and no one is on record as disagreeing in principle – although in practice, women today have generally not yet achieved the Halachic stature needed by poskim.[10]

Yet the fact that Halachah permits it did not stop the recent propagation of a novel argument against it. A Modern Orthodox rabbi based his objections to women *yoatzot halachah*[11] on an article in a Canadian newspaper. The article reportedly dealt with a female radiologist who had suddenly begun misinterpreting her data. She was found to be in the early stages of pregnancy; an excess of hormones had apparently affected her readings. Ergo, the rabbi argued, a woman cannot rule on Halachic matters, lest she be found to be in the early stages of pregnancy.

---

[5] *Orach Chayim 8:3.*

[6] Rema and Gra on *Yoreh Deah* 178:1. Another reason, even according to the Gra's approach, is that Biblical precedent can be found for women's dancing; and cf. *Bnei Banim* 2:30.

[7] *Mitzvah* 78 and 152.

[8] *Choshen Mishpat* 7:12.

[9] *Mitzvah* 78, end.

[10] Defined as those qualified to rule on new or difficult questions of Jewish law. The overwhelming majority of male rabbis have also not achieved this status.

[11] Women Halachic Advisors (not *poskot*) in the field of *hilchot Niddah.*

Anecdotes like this one are nonsensical "proof," but the above argument was made on a rabbis' internet list and has been repeated by others. Only an ideological blind spot in relation to women's issues can account for such a suspension of logic and common sense. And why stop at Halachah? By the same token, the advice of all women professionals – lawyers, physicians and others – may be in error and should not be relied upon, lest they be pregnant....

CHAPTER SEVEN

WOMEN'S HAIR COVERING AND DAILY PRAYERS

AS USED BY THE *POSKIM, limmud zechut* does not mean demonstrating the good intentions and sincerity of seeming violators of Halachah, but rather finding a source or argument to justify their apparently un-Halachic practices. Assumed, although not always articulated, is the proviso that the source or argument is a real one. A spurious or misinterpreted source is not a basis for *limmud zechut* any more than is *mutav she-yiheyu shogegin ve-al yiheyu mezidin*. It may be a mitigating factor in lieu of blame or punishment, but it does not justify the practice itself.

This applies, *inter alia,* to two recent topics of dispute. The first concerns a married woman's head-covering. A claim has been made that the *Shulchan Aruch* in *Even ha-Ezer* 115:4 holds that the prohibition of going outside wholly bareheaded is only a matter of custom, *dat Yehudit,* and therefore subject to change. Ignoring the improbability of the *Shulchan Aruch* holding a view that has no source in the *rishonim,* and the difficulty of reconciling such a ruling with the statement in the Talmud that going fully bareheaded is a *de-oraita* violation,[1] the claim hinges on the language of the *Shulchan Aruch*:

---

[1] See chap. 16 of my *Responsa on Contemporary Jewish Women's Issues* (Ktav, 2003).

What is *dat Yehudit?* It is a custom of modest behavior adopted by daughters of Israel. These are the things that, should she do any of them, she violates *dat Yehudit:* she goes out to market, or to an alleyway open on both ends or to a courtyard frequented by the public, *ve-rosha parua ve-ein aleha redid* like all women even though her hair is covered by a kerchief....

Does *"ve-rosha parua ve'ein aleha redid"* describe her as going out "when she is bareheaded *or* without a shawl over her..." – in which case the *Shulchan Aruch* classifies going bareheaded in the category of *dat Yehudit?* Or does it mean that she goes out "when she is bareheaded, without a shawl," i.e. with the phrase "without a shawl" being in apposition and explaining "bareheaded" – in which case going wholly bareheaded, without a shawl nor even a kerchief, is *not* subsumed under *dat Yehudit?*

Textual difficulties aside, what was not mentioned in the arguments on either side is that the entire paragraph starting from "What is...," except for the words "or to a courtyard frequented by the public" is a verbatim quote from the Rambam, *Hilchot Ishut* 24:12. The Rambam's meaning is patently the second of the above two interpretations, since in 24:11 he lists going completely bareheaded as *dat Moshe* (Mosaic law). Unless it can be demonstrated that the *Shulchan Aruch* is in the habit of using someone's exact language while meaning the opposite of what the original author intended, this would seem to settle the question: the *Shulchan Aruch* cannot mean that going completely bareheaded is only *dat Yehudit* – a notion, as mentioned, found nowhere in the *rishonim* – and, therefore, this cannot serve as a basis for *limmud zechut.*

The second controversy concerns the question of why most women do not recite *Shemoneh Esreh* regularly. *Magen Avraham* in *Orach Chayim* 106 explained that women rely on the Rambam, who holds that prayer is a Torah obligation met by any short, even self-composed prayer, and that the Sages did not otherwise obligate women in *Shemoneh Esreh*. The discussion revolves around whether the Rambam can be relied upon in the face of the disagreement of almost all other *rishonim*.

But is that really the opinion of the Rambam? In his commentary to the Mishnah in *Kiddushin* 1:7, concerning the principle that women are not obligated to observe "all" (i.e., any) positive commandments which are time-determined, Rambam writes:

> We have a generalization that one does not learn from generalizations, and by "all" they mean "most." The full range of positive commandments, those women are obligated in and those that they are not obligated in, are not subject to a generalization but rather are conveyed by oral tradition. Eating matzah on the night of *Pesach*, rejoicing on the Festival, *Hakhel*, prayer, reading the Megillah, Chanuka lights, Sabbath lights, and kiddush are all time-determined positive commandments, and in each of them men and women are equally obligated.

Here "prayer" (*tefilah*) clearly refers to the rabbinically-instituted *Shemoneh Esreh* prayer, which is time-determined and limited to specific hours, and not to the Torah obligation of prayer, which is not. That Rambam holds that women are rabbinically obligated in *Shemoneh Esreh* in addition to the Torah obligation can also be seen from his *Mishneh Torah,* by comparing the reference to "women, servants, and children" in *Hilchot Tefillah* 6:10 (the inclusion of children proves that he is referring to rabbinical prayer) with the reference to "women and servants" (but not children) in 1:2.

Finally, the Meiri in *Berachot* 20a, referring to the Rambam, writes that those who hold that women are obligated in prayer from the Torah hold that they are rabbinically obligated as well.

A mistaken reading of the Rambam cannot be used as grounds for *limmud zechut* for women not davening *Shemoneh Esreh*. But there exist other grounds for leniency. Women at the time of *Chazal* were not less burdened with having babies and raising children and running a household than they are today. How, then, could the Sages require women to daven *Shemoneh Esreh* regularly? Even if they tried to legislate it, would it not be in the category of an enactment that the community is unable to carry out, which is automatically null and void?

The answer, given by a number of modern writers, is that the original rabbinic enactment of *Shemoneh Esreh* included the provision that a person should not pray unless he can properly concentrate. The *Tur* in *Orach Chayim* 98 collected the various statements by *Chazal* in this regard:

> He should not pray in a place or time that negates his concentration, as R. Chiya b. Ashi said that Rav said, "Anyone whose thoughts are unsettled should not pray." R. Chanina did not pray on any day he got upset (*ratach*). R. Eliezer said, "Someone who returns from a journey should not pray for three days," i.e., until he is over the excitement of the trip. R. Eliezer b. R. Yose ha-Gelili said, "Nor one who is troubled (*metzar*)." Shmuel would not pray in a house where there was a brew because of the smell, which bothered him. R. Papa would not pray in a house where fish were frying.

None of this was codified in the *Shulchan Aruch* because, as the *Tur* himself wrote, at least since the time of R. Meir of Rottenberg in the thirteenth century the custom became established for men to pray even when not concentrating fully – lest they never pray at all. This custom, however, was adopted by the men but not by the women, who maintained the Talmudic exclusions.

The daily pressures, tensions and distractions involved in running a normal household and family thus enable most women to forgo *Shemoneh Esreh*. The upshot of this, however, is that unmarried students and other women, if they are living peaceful and unharried lives, are obligated in *Shemoneh Esreh* at least twice daily, *Shacharit* and *Minchah*.[2]

---

[2] On the question of the nightly *Arvit* prayer, see *Bnei Banim* vol. 2, no. 19, end.

CHAPTER EIGHT

BLESSING DAUGHTERS

*Y*ESIMECH *E*LOKIM *ke-Sarah, Rivkah, Rachel ve-Leah* (may G-d make you like Sarah, Rivkah, Rachel and Leah)," the blessing with which parents customarily bless their daughters on Friday evenings, first appeared in prayer books in the nineteenth century. It is not found in earlier editions such as R. Yaakov Emden's *Siddur Beit Yaakov* of 1748, which says only that

> It is a custom of Israel to bless the children (*ha-yeladim*) on Sabbath night. Those who bless say, "*Yesimcha Elokim ke-Efraim u-che-Menasheh* (may G-d make you like Efraim and like Menasheh)." (*Hanhagat Leil Shabbat*, 7)

Either the girls were not blessed at all or, what is more probable, they were blessed with Yaakov's blessing, "*Yesimcha Elokim ke-Efraim u-che-Menasheh*," just like the boys. After all, the Priestly blessing "May *ha-Shem* bless you and preserve you…" is also stated in the masculine but refers to both males and females.

At any rate, at some point the need was apparently felt for a distinctive blessing for daughters. But I have never been satisfied with the formula "*Yesimech Elokim ke-Sarah, Rivkah, Rachel ve-Leah*," for several reasons:

1. There is no source for it in Scripture or in the words of *Chaza"l*.

2. It is not parallel grammatically. It lacks the doubled letter *kaf* of "...*ke-Efraim u-che-Menasheh*."

3. It is not parallel in content. We do not bless the boys that they be like the three Patriarchs; why, then, bless the girls that they be like the four Matriarchs?

True, in *Sanhedrin* 105b the Sages expounded: "*'Mi-nashim ba-ohel tevorach'* (Judges 5:24) – who are they? Sarah, Rivkah, Rachel and Leah," but that only strengthens my argument. Were that the source for the Friday night blessing, we would bless our daughters by saying "*Mi-nashim ba-ohel tevorach*" or "*Tevorach ke-virkat Sarah, Rivkah, Rachel ve-Leah,*" or at least "*Yevarchech Elokim ke-Sarah, Rivkah, Rachel ve-Leah.*" Where does the current wording "*yesimech Elokim...*" come from? Clearly, from Yaakov's blessing of Efraim and Menasheh. The blessing of the daughters in current use, then, is a *cholent*.

For these reasons, my custom is to employ a blessing based on *Megillat Ruth* 4:11, which states: "All the people who were at the gate said, with the elders as witnesses: 'May *Elokim* grant that the woman who enters your house be like Rachel and like Leah, who together built the House of Israel." The blessing is, therefore, "*Yesimech (=yiten otach) Elokim ke-Rachel u-che-Leah, asher banu shetehen et Bet Yisrael.*"

This answers all the above objections. First, it has an explicit Scriptural source. Second, it is grammatically identical to the blessing of sons: "*ke-Efraim u-che-Menasheh*," "*ke-Rachel u-che-Leah*." Third and remarkably, the two blessings, for sons and for daughters, are similar in content. Scripture does not explain why it is a blessing to be like Efraim and Menasheh, but in all likelihood it is connected to the fact that they grew up together in brotherhood and harmony, unlike Yaakov's sons. So, too, Rachel and Leah grew up in sisterhood, as per the midrash that Rachel revealed her personal signs of identification to Leah to enable her to be married first.

My sons' blessing, then, is "*Yesimcha Elokim ke-Efraim u-che-Menasheh*," while my daughters' is "*Yesimech Elokim ke-Rachel u-che-Leah, asher banu shetehen et Bet Yisrael."* In the event, no Halachic problem is involved in changing the wording of non-mandatory blessings such as this one. One who is reluctant to part with the older version can even say them both, for as R. Emden wrote, "Everyone can add his own blessing, using his own formulation."

CHAPTER NINE

A MEMORIAL DAY FOR EUROPEAN JEWRY – AND DID ITS RABBIS ERR?

WHAT ONE *GADOL* WROTE in an article translated into English – that a separate memorial day for the victims of the Holocaust should not be established – is a legitimate viewpoint and deserves to be expressed. Not everyone agrees with it, however, and see Resp. *Seridei Eish*, part 2, no. 30 (note) who held that such a memorial day should indeed be established. Also, in my opinion, would that there were more memorial days, when Israeli theaters and nightclubs are closed! As *Kohelet* wrote, "It is better to go to the house of mourning…" (7:2).

In Resp. *Bnei Banim*, vol. 1 no. 10, I argued that one should stand during the siren on memorial days, and see vol. 2 no. 30 that *be-chukoteihem* does not apply to such standing, even according to the *Gra*. There I grouped the 27th day of Nisan (Holocaust Memorial Day) with the 4th day of Iyar (Memorial Day for Fallen Soldiers). Why should I distinguish between the two days? Is there anyone here who stands only on the 27th of Nisan but not on the 4th of Iyar, or vice versa?

Concerning the discussions of Holocaust Memorial Day, an article in *Ha-Ma'or* in 5741 argued at length that there is no prohibition involved, even *le-chatchilah*. By contrast, *Kovetz Igrot* of the *Chazon Ish*, chapter 97, deals specifically with a fast day and seven days of mourning, and not merely with a memorial day. Similarly, R. Feinstein zt"l in *Halacha u-Refu'ah*, vol. 5, p. 73, objected specifically to establishing a fast day. He brought proof from the lament recited on *Tisha be-Av* that "an additional date for [mourning the] destruction and conflagration should not be added"; one can argue with this, but in any case it does not pertain to a non-fast memorial day. In addition, the memorial days were established only in Israel for its citizens, and not for Jews around the world.

Had they consulted us we would not have counseled scheduling it during the month of Nisan, but it is not forbidden. The prohibition against reciting eulogies during the month of Nisan applies only during the initial seven days of mourning or, alternatively, during the first year; see *Yoreh Deah* 394 and *Orach Chayim* 547:5. Eulogies delivered two generations later are little more than simple remembrances, and are permitted.

Also, see *Bach* and *Chidushei Halachot* to *Tur Orach Chayim* 580, who distinguish between a fast day commemorating an event that already occurred on a particular day, which should therefore not be postponed, and between one established to pray that a disaster not occur in the future. They bring support for this distinction from *Sefer Rokeach*, chap. 212, who recorded that in Worms an annual fast day was established on *Rosh Chodesh* Sivan to recall a certain evil decree. It follows that one may also establish a memorial day on the 27th day of Nisan, in commemoration of the revolt in the Warsaw ghetto which took place around that date.

Bach made the above-mentioned distinction to explain the view of *Halachot Gedolot* that one may fast on the 1st of Nisan, in apparent contradiction to the Mishnah in *Ta'anit* 15a that prohibits one from fasting on *Rosh Chodesh*. He did not bother to explain another statement of *Halachot Gedolot,* that one fasts on the 25th of Nisan, in spite of the fact that according to *Masechet Soferim* 21:3–4 it is forbidden to fast or to eulogize during the entire month of Nisan. The reason is that both *Halachot Gedolot* and *Masechet Soferim* are Gaonic works, and neither is more authoritative than the other. According to *Halachot Gedolot*, then, during the month of Nisan there is no prohibition even against fasting, and while this is not the accepted Halachah, all would agree that it is permissible to establish a memorial day during Nisan without a fast.

The English article in question further sought to exonerate the *gedolim* of Europe of the charge that they failed to anticipate the Holocaust and did not encourage their communities to flee. Others have exerted themselves on this issue; for instance, some wrote that the Holocaust was a Heavenly decree from which it was impossible to escape. Still other Torah scholars were distressed by such claims and wrote that it would be better to keep silent about them.

Who will ascend to Heaven and return and tell us which view is correct? Regardless of the answer, I do not see what blame was incurred in not knowing the future. Where do we find that *gedolim* cannot err in matters affecting *klal Yisrael?* If not for errors we would still be living in our land and sacrificing in the Temple, as R. Yochanan said in *Gittin* 56a, "The forbearance of R. Zechariah b. Avkulis destroyed our home and burnt our sanctuary and exiled us from our land," because he lacked the prescience to prevent a war with Rome. In *Gittin* 56b the identical wording is used with regard to the "wicked empire," Rome, which "destroyed our home and burnt our sanctuary and exiled us from our land," and in *Berachot* 3a similar language is attributed to G-d in bemoaning Israel's sins. Taken together, it means that a number of factors joined in causing the destruction of the Second Temple: (a) the hostility of our enemies, (b) the mistakes of our leaders, and (c) our own sins. Because of (c), G-d did not intervene to save us from (a) and (b).

For that reason the Talmud in *Shabbat* 119b states that "Jerusalem would not have been destroyed" had its inhabitants not demeaned scholars, stopped children's Torah study, ceased reciting the *Shema*, profaned the Sabbath, refrained from admonishing each other and lacked a sense of shame, and similarly in *Bava Metzia* 30b. The Gemara does not say "Jerusalem was destroyed *because…*," for the potpourri of sins enabled the destruction to take place but did not cause it. See more in *Bnei Banim*, vol. 1, *maamar* 5.[1]

---

[1] Translated in my *Equality Lost* (Urim, 1999), chap. 12.

In *Gittin* 56b, R. Yochanan b. Zakai asked Vespasian, "Give me Yavne and its scholars." R. Yosef, and some say R. Akiva, applied to him the verse "Who turns back the wise and thwarts their opinions" because they thought he should have requested that he spare Jerusalem as well as Yavne. My grandfather *z"l* was distressed with R. Akiva for having been a factor in the destruction of Israel in the revolt of Bar Kochba. He explained the statement in *Menachot* 29b, "Such [he] arose in thought before Me," as meaning that R. Akiva himself raised the possibility of dying as a martyr, in order to atone for having contributed to Israel's destruction.

So, too, it was necessary for a king to inquire of the *Urim ve-Tummim* whether or not a war would be successful, even though permission to fight had already been granted by the Sanhedrin; see Rashi in *Berachot* 3b and *Sanhedrin* 17a. The agreement or advice of the Sanhedrin by itself was no guarantee that Israel would be victorious.

R. Zechariah b. Avkulis's poor judgment and that of others was a mistake rather than a sin. Similarly the inability of *gedolim* in Europe to anticipate the fate of their communities was a mistake rather than a sin.[2] Nor is it *lashon ha-ra* to recount the failings of R. Zechariah b. Avkulis, because of the importance of knowing that our leaders are not immune to the possibility of grievous error. Yet if we do not follow our leaders, whom shall we follow?

---

[2] According to Dr. Zerach Warhaftig *z"l*, who helped arrange the transfer of the Mir Yeshiva to Shanghai, he urged R. Aharon Kotler *z"l* to do the same for his yeshiva (Kletzk). R. Kotler demurred, believing that Lithuania, at the time neutral in the war, was in no danger. He even belittled the proffered travel documents, reportedly calling them "toilet paper." If this was indeed so, it was a fatal misjudgment but not a sin. Obviously, though, no one claims that any *gadol* or combination of *gedolim* could have saved European Jewry as a whole.

CHAPTER TEN

HONORING A *GADOL* WHO MALIGNS OTHERS

What of *"Yachid ve-rabim, halachah ke-rabim"?* He answered
that perhaps *Chazal* are telling us that only when the *'Yachid'*
– *Yechido shel Olam* (G-d) – is with the *rabim,* only then the
Halachah is with the *rabim.*

THIS *VORT* WAS QUOTED approvingly at a RIETS *Chag ha-Semicha* some years
ago. I am not a YU alumnus, but my wife is – with two degrees and an
honorary doctorate – and this was reported in an alumni magazine she
received. I wrote to the Rosh Yeshiva who quoted it that this was misguided
approval that would legitimize that *gadol's* path. The *gadol* and his followers
were the source of unprecedented personal defamation and vituperation of
other *gedolim* who did not share his views. These included even *gedolim* of
Agudas Israel – those of the Mizrachi, it goes without saying. According to
that *gadol,* they were heretics and doomed to hell for not sharing his
implacable opposition to any ties whatever to the State of Israel.

My grandfather *z"l* commented that in the time of the Temple, that *gadol*
would have been judged a *zaken mamre,* a deviant Elder. My grandfather, who
was both a *gadol ha-dor* and a *tzaddik ha-dor,* was not in the habit of speaking
ill of anybody. He was merely being factual. No one suggests that a *zaken*

mamre was a *rasha*. On the contrary, he was a great scholar, one worthy of belonging to the Sanhedrin. He was also clearly sincere, to the point that he was ready to die for what he thought was correct. But sincerity had nothing to do with it. He was an extreme individualist and a threat to the majority rule of Torah and was dealt with accordingly. No one suggested that R. Eliezer was a *rasha*, either, when they put him in *cherem* and announced that anything that he had ruled *tahor* should be treated as *tamei*.[1]

My grandfather's own attitude to the State of Israel deserves mention. He was strongly opposed to its establishment because he felt that a war would ensue and Jews would be killed.

After the State's establishment, however, he strongly supported it for the same reason: if there already was a State, if Jews did not support it there would be more war and Jews would be killed.[2]

For that reason he was at the time perhaps the only *gadol* who openly protested against those religious circles who, in the early 1950s, demonstrated against the State of Israel in front of its consulate in New York and through advertisements in the non-Jewish press. If *goyim* saw that even Jews were against the State, how could they be expected to support it? The result would be that more Jews would die. This practical approach was as far removed as could be imagined from the various ideological and theological positions of both supporters and opponents of Israel, then and now.

As a result of my grandfather's public stance he was denounced by zealots, some of whom reportedly went so far as to harass him via vituperative phone calls in the middle of the night, doing so even though at the time he was widely considered the *posek ha-dor* in North America.[3]

The *vort* served to justify an outspoken *gadol*'s dismissal of virtually the entire world of other *gedolim* and, I felt, should not be approvingly quoted to young *musmachim*. On the very real Halachic question of how such a *gadol*

---

[1] *Bava Metzia* 59b.

[2] See *Kitvei ha-Gri"a Henkin*, vol. 2, chap. 9.

[3] R. Feinstein, fourteen years younger, began to publish Resp. *Igrot Moshe* in 1959; R. Henkin was then almost eighty years old.

should himself be referred to — as *Mishneh la-Melech*[4] wrote, "Why are you concerned [only] for the honor of the one who denigrates? Be concerned for the honor of those who are denigrated!" — see *Bnei Banim* vol. 2, no. 34, in context of the question when must one say *zichrono li-vrachah* when mentioning a deceased scholar.

---

[4] *Hilchot Talmud Torah* 7:1.

CHAPTER ELEVEN

AFTER GUSH KATIF: MAY ONE OPPOSE ISRAEL'S GOVERNMENT?

THE EVENTS AT *GUSH KATIF* and at Amona[1] in 2005 raised questions such as: are current Israeli governments halachically legitimate? Can civil disobedience coexist with governmental authority? Does the need for protest outweigh the risk of disunity?

1.

Let me begin with recourse to the destruction of the Second Temple. The key Talmudic explanation of the second *churban* does not attribute it to sin. We read in *Yoma* (9b):

> Why was the first Temple destroyed? Because of three things which were present: idolatry, illicit sexual relations and murder.... But the Second Temple, [when] they were occupied with Torah, *mitzvot* and acts of kindness (*gemilut chassadim*) – why was it destroyed? Because of baseless hatred

---

[1] Six months after the destruction of Gush Katif, the evacuation of Amona was marked by unprecedented police violence.

which was present. To teach you that baseless hatred (*sinat chinam*) is equal to the three sins: idolatry, illicit sexual relations and murder.

The term "baseless hatred" requires clarification. Hatred is prohibited in *Vayikra* (19:17), "You shall not hate your brother in your heart," but this is not the *sinat chinam* the Gemara is referring to. The Torah refers to hatred "in your heart," i.e., surreptitious or masked enmity, whereas *sinat chinam* is not veiled at all. The Gemara quotes Ezekiel (21:7), "Groups [armed] with the sword were with my people," and explains, "These are men who eat and drink, and stab each other with verbal swords" – out loud and in public.

In *Vayikra* 19:18 the Torah commands, "Love your fellow as you do yourself," and R. Akiva considered this "a basic principle of the Torah." But violating this principle and refraining from acts of brotherly love and kindness is also not what the Gemara is referring to, for we read that during the Second Temple period people were occupied with "Torah, *mitzvot* and acts of kindness."

Underlying these difficulties is a fundamental problem. If *sinat chinam* refers to the *sin* of hatred, where is there Scriptural warning of punishment for such a sin? G-d does not punish without prior admonition. Nor is *sinat chinam* listed in *Avot* (5:9) among the sins which incur exile: "Exile is brought to the world by idolatry, by illicit sexual relations, by murder and by [non-observance of] the Sabbatical year." Similarly, in *Shabbat* (33a) the Sages said, "Because of the sins of idolatry, illicit sexual relations and murder and the abrogation of the Sabbatical and Jubilee years, exile is brought to the world and they [Israel] are exiled"; and also "because of the sin of murder the Temple is destroyed." They cited verses from the Torah which warn of the consequences of each of these sins. *Sinat chinam* is not mentioned.

The explanation is that the Talmud in *Yoma* does not cite *sinat chinam* in the context of sin and punishment.... "To teach you that baseless hatred is equal to the three sins of idolatry, illicit sexual relations and murder." It calls idolatry, illicit sexual relations and murder sins, but does not say "the *sin* of baseless hatred." Rather, *sinat chinam* refers to the internecine strife among the Jews, who quarreled with each other instead of uniting against the

Romans. Rabbeinu Chananel in *Yoma* comments that "had they ascended together like a wall" they would not have been crushed, and Maharsha cites an example of factionalism and its consequences. Because of baseless hatred and disunity, the Temple was destroyed and we were exiled.

We can now understand the statement, "to teach you that baseless hatred is equal to the three sins: idolatry, illicit sexual relations and murder." It would indeed be astonishing to equate the three cardinal sins, concerning which Halachah demands that one give up one's life rather than violate them and which carry the death penalty, with the relatively minor sin of hatred which is not even punishable by the lash. Rather, the term "is equal to *(shekulah ke-neged)*" in the Talmud involves a comparison of another sort:

1. Either that certain *mitzvot* are preconditions for or lead to the observance of all the others, as the Torah states concerning *tzitzit:* "You will see it and remember all *haShem's mitzvot* and do them" (*Bamidbar* 15:39).

2. Or that they have similar results even though they work in different ways, as the *Sifrei* in *parshat Re'eh* says "Dwelling in the Land of Israel is equal to all the commandments." Observing *mitzvot* in the aggregate leads to awareness of G-d, as does dwelling in Israel, as stated in *Ketubbot* (110b), "Everyone who lives in the Land of Israel is as if he has a Deity, as it is written, '...to give you the land of Canaan, to be your G-d'" (*Vayikra* 25:38).

In this sense, *sinat chinam* is indeed equal to idolatry, illicit sexual relations and murder: it brought about the destruction of the Second Temple just as surely as the three sins brought about the destruction of the First, albeit in very different ways.

2.

In view of the above, should we not have given in at the confrontation at Amona? Should we not give in during future confrontations as well, in order to avoid *sinat chinam* and a rift in the nation? Even if the government violates

Halachah, is not *sakanta* (danger) halachically more serious than *issura* (prohibition)[2] and, in this case, should we not place avoiding the dangers of a rift above all other considerations?

It seems to me, however, that it is not possible to decide our question on the basis of possible *sakanta*. Those who oppose the evacuation of settlements claim that the government's policy of territorial concessions to the Arabs without any return poses an existential danger to the state – as proven by subsequent events in Gaza and, more recently, by the war in Lebanon – no less critical than the danger of a rift in the nation. Plus, it is the government that fostered the rift by inciting public opinion against religious Zionism in general and against the settlers in particular. For their part, those who supported disengagement pointed to serious, long-term demographic dangers from incorporating millions of Palestinians into Israel.

Generals and other experts are to be found on both sides of the controversy. And while governments have the right to establish their own policies, in basic questions of defense and foreseeing the future they often have no superior knowledge. Thus it is that basic policy can change overnight with new elections: the presuppositions brought to power largely determine the reading of events.

Nor, in matters of leadership, do simple rules of Halachic decision-making apply. For example, R. Yochanan, in *Gittin* 56a, placed the blame for the destruction of the Temple on the failed leadership of R. Zechariah b. Avkulis, because of the latter's indecision in the affair of bar Kamtza. Yet in that same tractate of *Gittin*,[3] R. Yochanan twice declared that in halachic matters, when unsure it is better to do nothing. Refusing to act when in doubt is good Halachah, but may be perilous statecraft!

Similarly, R. Yochanan introduced the account of R. Zechariah b. Avkulis and Bar Kamtza by quoting a verse from *Mishlei* (28:5), "Fortunate is the man who is always afraid, and he who hardens his heart will fall into evil." According to R. Yochanan, what must one be afraid of?

---

[2] *Chullin* 10a.

[3] 19a and 37a: "*Ve-chi mi-pnei she-mi-daminan, naaseh maaseh?*"

I think the answer is to be found in the one other place in the Talmud where the verse "Fortunate is the man…" is cited. In tractate *Berachot* 60a we read:

> A student was walking behind R. Yishmael b. R. Yosi in the Zion market. He saw that the student was afraid. He said to him, "You are a sinner, as it is written, 'Sinners are afraid in Zion' (Isaiah 32:14)." – But is it not (also) written, "Fortunate is the man who is always afraid"? That applies to matters of Torah.

Rashi explained "that applies to matters of Torah" as meaning that one should be afraid of forgetting what he learned, but the second half of the verse "and one who hardens his heart will fall into evil" does not seem to indicate this. Following the words of R. Yochanan, it appears that the explanation is, rather: fortunate is the man who is afraid lest he has not properly grasped the Torah he has learned, lest he draw mistaken conclusions from it, as did R. Zechariah b. Avkulis, who undoubtedly derived a Torah precedent from somewhere for not deciding in the affair of Bar Kamtza[4]; nevertheless, R. Yochanan blamed him for the destruction of the Temple.

3.

Regarding civil disobedience, even a nonreligious Israeli government has much of the halachic authority of monarchy. As Responsa *Tzitz Eliezer* (10:1:14) wrote:

> In our day as well, the president and the government and the Knesset (with all their limitations in the area of religion – it is clear that with regard to religion, their decisions against it have no validity whatsoever) which were elected by a Jewish majority living in its land… stand in place of a king in

---

[4] For discussion of this and other aspects of the destruction of the Second Temple, see my *Equality Lost*, chapter 12.

everything touching on the general circumstances of the nation.

Indeed, although the Ten Tribes worshipped idols, nevertheless the Jerusalem Talmud states, "A king [of the Kingdom] of Israel and a king of the House of David are both equal [in their standing as kings]..." (*Horayot* 3:2). Nor can it be claimed that prophets anointed all the kings of Israel. There is no mention of a prophet appointing any of the kings of the House of Omri, as *Tosafot*[5] notes, and yet Elijah ran before Achav in his honor.

Similarly, although wicked or illegitimate kings ruled in the time of the Second Temple, we do not find that their reigns were not recognized after the fact. For example, King Agrippas I was halachically ineligible for the monarchy because he came from a family of converts; nevertheless, he read from the Torah at *Hakhel* as befitted a king, and the Sages praised him for it (*Sotah* 41a).

Since the government has the rights and authority of *malchut*/kingship, does one who agitates against government policy violate a Halachic prohibition? I think the answer to this question hinges on the differences between the Rambam's *Sefer ha-Mitzvot* and his *Mishneh Torah* concerning the rights of kings. In *Sefer ha-Mitzvot* (*Aseh* 173), Rambam wrote:

> When the king issues a command that does not violate the Torah, there is an obligation to obey his command, and one who violates his command and does not fulfill it – the king has permission to kill him.

Two separate laws are listed here: first, there is an obligation to carry out the commands of the king, and second, the king has permission to kill anyone who does not obey him. The source for both of these is undoubtedly the first chapter of the Book of Joshua. In verse 17, the people committed themselves to obeying Yehoshua, "In the same way that we obeyed Moshe, we will obey you," and in verse 18 they authorized him to kill anyone who

---

[5] *Sanhedrin* 20b, *s.v. Melech.*

did not carry out his commands: "Any man who violates your orders... will be put to death."

However, the Talmud in Tractate *Sanhedrin* (49a) cites as Halachah only verse 18 – nowhere is verse 17 cited.[6] So, too, Rambam in *Hilchot Melachim* 3:8 writes, "Anyone who rebels against the king – the king has permission to kill him," in conformance with the latter verse, while omitting mention of a personal obligation to obey the king's commands as per the earlier verse. The implication is that, although a king and, by extension, a government has the right to enforce obedience to its policies, there is no Halachic violation involved in the very act of opposing those same policies. And, although if disobeying a king or a government were to put one in imminent danger of death it would be forbidden to disobey, such a possibility does not exist in western countries today.

Even though in *Hilchot Melachim* 4:1 Rambam did write that it is forbidden (*assur*) to circumvent customs duties because they belong to the king, there is a great difference between financial obligations and general obedience. Certainly it is forbidden to steal from the king or government – just as it is prohibited to steal from anyone – and this prohibition is independent of the presence or absence of any danger.

A further distinction between *Sefer ha-Mitzvot* and *Hilchot Melachim* is that in the former, Rambam limited the authority to execute rebels to a king "appointed according to the Torah," following the precedent of Yehoshua. Such authority would not devolve on today's governments, none of which are appointed "according to the Torah." Rambam did not, however, codify this condition in his *Mishneh Torah*.[7] Thus, today's governments retain the powers listed in *parshat ha-melech* in I Samuel chap. 8, following Rambam's ruling that a king is authorized to carry out everything written in that

---

[6] Perhaps the reason is that verse 18 is conditioned on "only be strong and of good courage," a condition which has been met by rulers throughout history. Verse 17, on the other hand, is conditioned on "only be *haShem* with you as He was with Moshe" which was fulfilled in the case of Yehoshua alone, as G-d promised him in verse 5: "As I was with Moshe, so I will be with you...."

[7] See *Bnei Banim*, vol. 3, no. 33, p. 112.

chapter. But there is no mention in I Samuel or elsewhere in Scripture of any personal obligation to obey a king, only that the king is entitled to enforce his prerogatives.

The upshot of this is that whether according to *Sefer ha-Mitzvot*, which mentions an obligation to obey the king on pain of death but conditions this on his being appointed according to the Torah, or according to the *Mishneh Torah* which neither mentions such an obligation nor makes such a condition – according to Rambam, there is no intrinsic prohibition of civil disobedience in opposing the policies of today's governments, as long as the protests themselves do not violate Halachah.

4.

Another possible factor is *dina de-malchuta dina*, "the law of the kingdom is law," which mandates conformity to the law of the land. This is a topic with many divergent approaches and disagreements among the *Rishonim*. Nevertheless, one may point to several aspects, each of which has wide support among the *poskim*, although there is no unanimity – other than that *dina de-malchuta dina* does not apply when the government commands violation of Halachah.[8]

> a) The law of the "kingdom" is the law, not the law of the king.

As Responsa Rashba (6:254) puts it:

> Every nation has known laws, and laws *de-malchuta* (of the kingdom) was said, laws *de-malka* (of the king) was not said. Everything which is not part of the laws of the kingdom is not the law, even if the king now decrees it.

That is to say, only laws which are in accordance with the legislative tradition of the particular country are subsumed under *dina de-malchuta dina*, while whatever the king innovates which was not accepted law beforehand,

---

[8] See *Bnei Banim*, vol. 2, no. 52 and in *Akdamot* 18, pp. 93–95.

is only *dina de-malka,* a law of a particular king, and is not independently Halachically binding. Perhaps *chaza"l* wished to avoid giving sanction to governmental whims, as per Ahasuerus who issued decrees and then changed his mind, and therefore they included in *dina de-malchuta dina* only laws which are firmly entrenched.

One may wonder whether there was any *dina de-malka* greater than the disengagement legislation: the former prime minister initiated it by himself and in opposition to everything that he and previous governments had thought, done and adhered to.

b)   Equitable legislation (*dina*), not *gezeilah* (robbery), is the law.

As opposed to the previous opinion, according to many *Rishonim* including the *Tur* (*Choshen Mishpat* 369) *dina de-malchuta dina* applies to new legislation as well as established laws, but only on condition that the whole population is treated equally. An inequitable law is not subject to *dina de-malchuta dina,* and even a majority has no right to rob and oppress a minority. The disengagement legislation discriminated against one sector of the population. The compensation offered did not meet accepted standards pertaining to expropriation of lands and demolishing homes in the rest of the country.

In addition, it can be inferred from the discussions of many *Rishonim* that *dina de-malchuta dina* applies only to monetary matters, in contrast to the notion that one who crosses the street when the light is red or exceeds the speed limit violates *dina de-malchuta dina* in addition to the prohibition against endangering oneself. Indicative is the fact that all four places in the Talmud[9] that mention *dina de-malchuta dina* deal with monetary matters. For that reason, as well, the wording is *dina* (monetary law) *de-malchuta dina* and not *issura* (prohibition) *de-malchuta issura* or *chiyuva* (obligation) *de-malchuta chiyuva.*

---

[9] *Nedarim* 28a, *Gittin* 10b, *Bava Kama* 103a, *Bava Metzia* 54b.

5.

It is difficult to formulate the precise boundaries of permitted protest. However, those who believe that the policy of disengagement represents an existential danger to the State of Israel and its people will not be absolved of responsibility if they take no action to prevent it. In such things one must follow one's conscience.

One need not wonder at the fact that there are no clear guidelines for this. Complex problems do not admit of easy solutions. Similarly, there are no clear guidelines to the obligation of "it is time to act for *ha-Shem*" (*Berachot* 54a). There the need is to act for *ha-Shem*, and here the need is to act for one's people and one's country.

Proverbs (24:11–12) applies to those who recognize the danger in their hearts, but remain aloof:

> Save those taken to death, and hold back those approaching slaughter. If you say, "We did not know this" – does not He understand what is innermost in hearts? And He who guards your soul, He knows, and will repay a person according to his deeds.

CHAPTER TWELVE

HOMOSEXUALITY, SIN AND *TINOK SHE-NISHBA*

THE HEAD OF A YESHIVA I studied at was asked permission to conduct a survey of the religious beliefs and practices of his students. The questionnaire included the query, "Do you believe in G-d?" and the *rosh yeshiva* declined permission. He was concerned lest some students ponder the question and conclude, "Well, actually, no!" Translated into terms of a different topic, it is not our responsibility to insure that a youth with homosexual tendencies will be honest with himself if such honesty will lead him from homosexual tendencies to homosexual practice.

A man with overtly homosexual behavior, on the other hand, should not be pressured into attempting marriage. As ruled by Rema in *Even ha-Ezer* 1:3, today the *bet din* no longer coerces anyone to marry, and while this certainly does not free one from the obligation of non-coercive *tochecha* – urging and encouraging others to fulfill the *mitzvah* of procreation – there is nothing to be gained by advocating the impossible or the highly improbable.

Also, Rabbeinu Yonah, in *Igeret ha-Teshuvah,* lists giving proper advice as part of the mitzvah of *gemilut chessed.* Full advance disclosure to the prospective bride is Halachically mandatory and would prevent such a marriage. Unfortunately, such disclosure may be ignored in favor of a conspiracy of silence on the part of a homosexual *chatan* and his friends, in the misguided hope that things will somehow work themselves out in marriage.

The statement "Judaism looks negatively at homosexual activity, not at the homosexual" mirrors the famous comment by Bruriah in *Berachot* 10a that the Torah seeks the extirpation of the sin and not of the sinner. Until recently, Judaism's opposition to homosexual activity was unquestioned and matched by that of society in general, and it was the second half of the above statement that needed emphasizing. However, there are campuses today where the influence of gay/lesbian groups is such that those who eschew experimentation with homosexuality find themselves under peer pressure. For Jewish students exposed to such a climate, it is often opposition to homosexuality itself that needs reinforcement.

For that and other reasons there is something to be said for the utility of abhorrence as a barrier against homosexuality, regardless of how one understands the Biblical term *to'evah* and in spite of the risks of confusing the sin with the sinner. It is, alas, only a pale remnant of the visceral reaction against sin in general *(yir'at chet)*, which was once more prevalent than it is today.

On the subject of *tinok she-nishba,* a Jewish child brought up among the nations without knowledge of his background: originally, *tinok she-nishba* was a transient status – once a person found out that he was Jewish and that Jews observed the Torah, he was no longer a *tinok she-nishba.* It was axiomatic that birth into a community entailed following the practices of that community; therefore, it was enough to discover one's real identity in order to be bound by it. There are still echoes of this today, as in those survivors of the Holocaust who were raised from infancy as Catholics and whose discovery at a later age that they had been born Jewish started them on the road back to Judaism.

Once he discovered who he was, a *tinok she-nishba* could not continue to plead ignorance. If he did not know the details of Judaism – for example, that there was such a thing as *Shabbat* – it was now his responsibility to go and learn them. This presupposed that there was only one recognized version of Judaism. If rival claims existed, as in the case of the Karaites, how was the *tinok she-nishba* to know what version of Judaism he was supposed to adopt? This was the background to the Rambam's transforming *tinok she-nishba* into a permanent status, transferable from one generation to the next.[1]

It took recent generations to apply the concept of *tinok she-nishba* to simple backsliding, even in the absence of a competing religious claim. The problem with this expanded application of *tinok she-nishba* is that it can be misused to justify or exonerate everything and anything. The worshippers of the Golden Calf? Why, they were all *tinokot she-nishbu* as slaves in Egypt. The worshippers of Ba'al? *Tinokot she-nishbu* on account of the pervasive Canaanite influence in the region!

Taken at face value, some other Talmudic statements can also be misemployed to free the individual from responsibility for his actions. In *Sotah* 3a, "No one violates a prohibition unless he is first possessed by a craze *(ruach shel shtut)*." Or in *Yoma* 86a, "If one violates a prohibition and repeats it, it [then] seems to him to be permitted." One who is temporarily crazed or who believes that what he does is acceptable, is hardly culpable, nor is someone whose beliefs and behavior can be completely attributed to his upbringing and environment. And while the above are non-Halachic formulations, *Tosafot* in *Sanhedrin* 9b refer to someone as being "coerced *(anoos)* by his sexual inclinations."

As Orthodox Jews today cast the net of *tinok she-nishba* wider and wider, using it to exonerate increasingly larger circles of Jewish society, they run the risk of the ultimate corruption: applying the concept of *tinok she-nishba* to *themselves*, thereby eradicating any sense of guilt and precluding the need for and possibility of *teshuvah*. That is the prospect that gives one pause, even as one supports every individual display of graciousness shown to those who suffer from being homosexuals.

---

[1] *Hilchot Mamrim* 3:3.

AFTERWORD: ON THE YAHRZEIT OF R. YOSEF ELIYAHU HENKIN ZT"L

AMONG MANY PERSONAL memories I have of him are two concerning women. The first is that in *birkat ha-mazon* his wife read the *"ha-rachaman"* section out loud and he answered amen. Why? To give her *nachat ruach* (satisfaction). The second is from after the Pesach seder a year before his passing. My wife told him how much she enjoyed his tune for *chasal siddur Pesach*. He replied that he had learned it from the *Ridbaz* in Slutzk, and sang it for her over again from beginning to end.

And an incident told to me by R. Avraham Price *z"l* of Toronto, the author of *Mishnat Avraham:* it was on a winter morning in a synagogue in Manhattan. Barely a minyan was present; it was frigid and blustery, and R. Price said that had he not had to say *kaddish* he would have stayed home. The door blew open and in walked R. Henkin. He had come to collect for Ezras Torah, the charity he headed, and he collected a few dollars. R. Price asked him: for a couple of dollars, did he really have to go out in such weather? R. Henkin answered: "R. Price, I'm surprised at you. It's my employment. Am I supposed to receive a salary for nothing?"

Twenty years ago I had the privilege of visiting Orthodox communities throughout the United States and Canada. In one city after another I heard from elderly rabbis: R. Henkin said this. R. Henkin ruled that. R. Henkin determined the name of the city and enabled us to write *gittin*. In the 1940s and 1950s and beyond, his rulings were cited in thousands of homes across North America.

At a memorial gathering held in Jerusalem thirty days after his death in 5733, six prominent *roshei yeshiva* spoke. All of the yeshivot in Israel and their students received support from Ezras Torah, and the *bet midrash* of the Chebiner Yeshiva was full. The first *rosh yeshiva* finished speaking, and shortly afterwards got up and left, followed by his students. The second *rosh yeshiva* spoke at length and he, too, left with his students. And so on, until at the end only a few people remained. At that point I spoke on behalf of the family, as a grandson who had learned with R. Henkin for many years.

Today, not thirty days but thirty-four years since his passing, how are we to evaluate the life and work of my grandfather, the *gaon* and *tzaddik*, R. Yosef Eliyahu Henkin? A generation has arisen "who knew not Yosef." Occasionally I've read discussions citing the Halachic opinions of rabbis and *roshei yeshiva* in the United States before and after World War II, with the writers being unaware of who was the primary address for Halachic decisions at the time.

But even if details are sometimes forgotten, everyone knows that indeed there lived such a sage, ranked among the great rabbis of every generation. For those who recall his qualities, a unique blend of great Torah scholarship and unassuming Halachic authority with fearlessness and originality, and of decisiveness tempered by humility and innumerable acts of *chessed* and devotion to the community, his memory and his example still serve as an inspiration and a guide in life. His memory is a blessing. Would that we had his like today.

For a biography of R. Yosef Eliyahu Henkin, *zt"l*, see *Equality Lost*, chap. 16.

GLOSSARY (CHAPTERS 4–12)

Chapter 4

Arayot – illicit sexual relationships (sing. *ervah*)

Aseh – positive Torah commandment

Lo ta'aseh – negative Torah commandment

Niddah – menstruating woman

Shomer negiah – one who refrains from touching members of the opposite sex other than one's spouse and close family members

Yehareg ve-al ya'avor – the principle that there are commandments that one should be killed rather than violate

Chapter 5

Aliyot – calling up to the reading of the Torah (sing. *aliyah*)

Ba'al keriah – actual Torah reader

Birkat ha-mazon – Grace after meals

Chumashim – incomplete Torah scrolls

Heter – permissive ruling

Kevod (ha-)tzibbur – the honor of the congregation

Sha'at ha-dechak – straitened circumstances

Chapter 6

Be-chukoteihem – [Torah prohibition against following] the ways of other nations

Ma'aseh – act, deed

Shev ve-al ta'aseh – refrain from action

Ta'am – reason

Chapter 7

Chazal – the Talmudic Sages

Dat Moshe – Mosaic law

Dat Yehudit – Judaic law (custom)

De-oraita – of the Torah

Limmud zechut – adducing merit

Minchah – afternoon prayer

Mutav she-yiheyu shogegin ve-al yiheyu mizidin – better they be mistaken violators
than willful sinners

Rishonim – early, medieval Torah authorities

Shacharit – morning prayer

Shemoneh Esreh – "the Eighteen Blessings," the principal part of the daily
prayer service

Chapter 8

Cholent – a stew (Yid.); a hodge-podge

Chapter 9

Gadol – Torah authority (pl. *gedolim*)

Lashon ha-ra – forbidden speech, such as gossip or tale-bearing

Chapter 10

Chag ha-Semicha – ceremony ordaining new rabbis

Cherem – excommunication

Ha-dor – [of] the generation

Musmachim – newly ordained rabbis

Rabim – many

Rasha – wicked person

RIETS – the R. Isaac Elchanan Theological Seminary at Yeshiva University

Tahor – pure

Tameh – impure

Vort – (Yid.) short Torah homily

Yachid – individual

Zichrono li-vracha – may his memory be a blessing

Chapter 11

Hakhel – septennial Torah reading in the Temple

Chapter 12

Chatan – bridegroom

Teshuvah – repentance

Rabbi Yehuda Henkin, an authority on Jewish law *(posek halacha)*, occupies a central position in contemporary halachik discourse. The author of *Bnei Banim* – four volumes of Hebrew responsa – and a commentary on the Torah, he also writes prolifically in English on topics of Torah commentary, halacha and Jewish thought. He is the grandson of the gaon Rabbi Yosef Eliyahu Henkin *ztz"l*.

Rabbi Henkin's previous books in English are: Equality Lost: Essays in Torah Commentary, Halacha, and Jewish Thought (Urim, 1999), New Interpretations on the Parsha (Ktav, 2001), and Responsa on Contemporary Jewish Women's Issues (Ktav, 2003).